D0092112

THE FIELDS OF PRAISE

THE FIELDS OF PRAISE

NEW AND SELECTED POEMS

MARILYN NELSON

LOUISIANA STATE UNIVERSITY PRESS
Baton Rouge and London   1997

Designer: Amanda McDonald Key
Typeface: Sabon
Printer and binder: Thomson-Shore, Inc.

ISBN 0-8071-2174-6 (cl : alk. paper). —ISBN 0-8071-2175-4 (p : alk. paper)

The paper in this book meets the guidelines for permanence and durability of
the Committee on Production Guidelines for Book Longevity of the Council
on Library Resources. ♾

The author gratefully acknowledges the editors of the following publications,
in which some of the new poems first appeared: *Gettysburg Review* ("Is She
Okay?" "Fish and Floor-Dust Bouquet"), *Southern Review* ("The Death of
Polyxena," "Hecuba Mourns"), *Oxford Magazine* ("Beauty Shoppe," "Like
Father, Like Son"), *Texas Observer* ("Photographs of the Medusa," "Men in
the Kitchen"), *American Poetry Review* ("Blessing the Boats"), *Kenyon
Review* ("Post-Prandial Conversation"), *Crab Orchard Review* ("Leaving the
Hospice"), *North Atlantic Review* ("As Simple as That"), *Chattahoochee
Review* ("Impala"), *Obsidian II* ("Minor Miracle"), *Philomathean Society
Anthology of Poetry in Honor of Daniel Hoffman* ("Boys in the Park"), and
1996 Frost Place Anthology ("Clown Nose").

To Jacob and Dora

CONTENTS

II / HOMEPLACE

I I I / H E R M I T A G E

IV / STILL FAITH

ACKNOWLEDGMENTS

*My thanks to my dear friends and members of my
family, as well as to Thorkild Bjørnvig, Drew Black-
well, Bob Deppe, Jay Derringer, Rita Dove, Martin Es-
pada and the Third World Villanelle Society, Margaret
Gibson, Marilyn Hacker, Kurt Juul, Inge Pedersen,
Don Sheehan, and Erdmann Waniek.*

*I'm especially grateful to my friend Pamela Espe-
land for her thoughtful and thorough editing of this
manuscript.*

I don't know how my mother walked her troubles down.
I don't know how my father stood his ground.
I don't know how my people survived slavery.
I do remember, that's why I believe.

Sweet Honey in the Rock

I

MAMA AND DADDY

COVER PHOTOGRAPH

I want to be remembered
with big bare arms akimbo
and feet splay-toed and flat arched
on the welcome mat of dirt.

I want to be remembered
as a voice that was made to be singing
the lullaby of shadows
as a child fades into a dream.

I want to be as familiar
as the woman in the background
when the heroine is packing
and the Yankee soldiers come.

Hair covered with a bandanna,
I want to be remembered
as an autumn under maples:
a show of incredible leaves.

I want to be remembered
with breasts that never look empty,
with a childbearing, generous waistline
and with generous, lovemaking hips.

I want to be remembered
with a dark face absorbing all colors
and giving them back twice as brightly,
like water remembering light.

I want to be remembered
with a simple name, like Mama:
as an open door from creation,
as a picture of someone you know.

(Mama's Promises)

WILD PANSIES

for Mandy Jordan

I rested in my mother's womb,
a lily on the pond.
Gentle waves moved the water;
I rocked, held by a twisted cord
of roots.
From the moment I was planted there
I thought about learning to walk
more than nine months
before I was born.

I listened to the voices
of the water around me;
sometimes I thought a storm
was really three hearts
beating as one.

I grew from a bundle of jelly-eggs
into a tadpole nosing the water weeds.
Then I was the size of a rainbow trout,
and then I was me.

I jumped up the falls
of the birth canal
and knew, as my body
hit sunlight,
what it would feel like to fly.
But when I got to the top
I could breathe water no more.

Before I drew dry air
for the first time
into my lungs,
I said to myself, Remember.

How the pine trees
shadowed the water
when evening came.
How the sunset was reflected.
How the wild pansies
grew along the shore.

(Mama's Promises)

MY SECOND BIRTH

That first birth
when I pushed myself
free of her
and burst out
into invisible air
is as lost to me
as the months I floated
in that ocean of unbroken thought.

But passing on
the birth she gave me
has made me see Mama
face to face.

I understand now
what she means when she says
she loves me:
It's the place you get to
when you've pushed
to the other side of pain.

A light grew in my belly
until my husband
could warm his hands by it.
I gave our son my broken sleep,
the fists, hands, fists, hands, fists
I made when he woke me
from my dream about his name.

I gave birth to him awed
by his apple-round head
in the bright glass above my knees.
I was given new strength
when he crowned
and my blood burst

like a chain of jewels
around his neck.

Mama
was my first image of God.
I remember how she leaned over my crib,
her eyes full of sky.

(Mama's Promises)

THE LOST DAUGHTER

One morning just before Christmas
when I was four or five years old
I followed Mama's muskrat coat
and her burgundy cloche
from counter to counter in The May Co.
as she tested powders and colognes,
smoothed silk scarves and woolen vests,
and disappeared down the aisle
into the life she lived before I was born.

The mirrors rendered nothing more
at my eye level than a small brown blur;
I understood why the salesclerks didn't see
a little girl in a chesterfield coat,
plaid bows on her five skimpy braids,
or stop me as I wept my way
toward the outside doors
and was spun through their transparency
out into the snow.

On the sidewalk Santa rang a shiny bell
and shifted from his right boot to his left
as the fingers in my mittens froze
and fell off, one by one.
My skin, then my bones turned to stone
that parted the hurrying crowd,
until at last I drifted, thinned as the smoke
from an occasional pipe or cigarette,
through the thick white words people spoke.

Sometimes a taxi squealed its brakes
or beeped to pierce the solid, steady roar
of voices, wheels, and motors.
The same blue as the sky by now,

I rose like a float in the parade
I'd seen not long before:
a mouse tall as a department store
that nodded hugely as it moved
above our wonder down the avenue.

When Mama spat out my name
in fury and relief, I felt my face
fly back into focus. I formed again
instantaneously under her glaring eyes.
In the plate glass window I recognized
the shape Mama shook and embraced—
the runny nose, the eyes' frightened gleam,
the beret askew on hair gone wild—
and knew myself made whole again, her child.

(Mama's Promises)

A STRANGE BEAUTIFUL WOMAN

A strange beautiful woman
met me in the mirror
the other night.
Hey,
I said,
What you doing here?
She asked me
the same thing.

(Mama's Promises)

MAMA'S PROMISE

I have no answer to the blank inequity
of a four-year-old dying of cancer.
I saw her on TV and wept
with my mouth full of meatloaf.

I constantly flash on disasters now;
red lights shout *Warning. Danger.*
everywhere I look.
I buckle him in, but what if a car
with a grille like a sharkbite
roared up out of the road?
I feed him square meals,
but what if the fist of his heart
should simply fall open?
I carried him safely
as long as I could,
but now he's a runaway
on the dangerous highway.
Warning. Danger.
I've started to pray.

But the dangerous highway
curves through blue evenings
when I hold his yielding hand
and snip his minuscule nails
with my vicious-looking scissors.
I carry him around
like an egg in a spoon,
and I remember a porcelain fawn,
a best friend's trust,
my broken faith in myself.
It's not my grace that keeps me erect
as the sidewalk clatters downhill
under my rollerskate wheels.

Sometimes I lie awake
troubled by this thought:

It's not so simple to give a child birth;
you also have to give it death,
the jealous fairy's christening gift.

I've always pictured my own death
as a closed door,
a black room,
a breathless leap from the mountaintop
with time to throw out my arms, lift my head,
and see, in the instant my heart stops,
a whole galaxy of blue.
I imagined I'd forget,
in the cessation of feeling,
while the guilt of my lifetime floated away
like a nylon nightgown,
and that I'd fall into clean, fresh forgiveness.

Ah, but the death I've given away
is more mine than the one I've kept:
from my hands the poisoned apple,
from my bow the mistletoe dart.

Then I think of Mama,
her bountiful breasts.
When I was a child, I really swear,
Mama's kisses could heal.
I remember her promise,
and whisper it over my sweet son's sleep:

> *When you float to the bottom, child,*
> *like a mote down a sunbeam,*
> *you'll see me from a trillion miles away:*
> *my eyes looking up to you,*
> *my arms outstretched for you like night.*

(Mama's Promises)

I DECIDE NOT TO HAVE CHILDREN

Dawn, the gulls weep for the Jews,
and up through my muddy blood
my lost sister rises like a drowned puppy.
I'd forgotten how far away
I'd sent her, wonder how it was
in that wet country,
her skin melting back into mine.
There were nights
I almost recognized her face,
like an old rose pressed under glass.
Sometimes she made
a knock in the pipes
faint as a heartbeat
and backed away again.

In some small room of myself
she has shrunk
to the size of a sparrow
since the night the soldiers came
and searched through my dreams
in their angry uniforms.
I find her there, halfway to sleep,
a sister smaller than a hare
in the blind appendix
behind my eyes.

I'd forgotten how much I cared
and she comes holding out
her fat brown fists,
the flowers of mourning
already twisted in her hair.
Her faint body made a light
that warmed the whole house.

(For the Body)

MAMA I REMEMBER

Mama I remember.
My hair was in braids—
you tapped done with the comb
and I stood up between your knees.
You were always
packing for the movers,
sitting in front of me
when I touched my father's hair.
You never cried,
wrapped glasses in newspaper,
took the pictures down.
The last baby grew
warped in your womb,
smiled three years
and died. I remember
your eyes when you climbed
into the ambulance.
You patted my cheek,
your hands wet with blood.

You stared
when I slapped the wall
and cursed the hospital
where my father died.
Now you meditate.
I understand
your need, the soft ache
of loss in your thighs.

(For the Body)

Her leg flies open like a dictionary dropped,
the white fat sickens her till her blood
fills the wound, and I, dumb with terror,
run away from the gully gaudy with broken glass
while my sister's scream shrinks to child size
at my cowardly back. A white door opens
as my fists blur on the wood.
The white lady who takes me in
has no age, has no face, only a voice
from somewhere else that asks my mother's name
over the rip of clean sheets.
Jennifer comes alone up the forbidden trail,
leaving bloody footprints in the snow.

Five-fifty on a wet October morning.
I'm awake now, still running home to get Mama,
confession still cold on my tongue.
I sit up in the dark. I count my murders.

> My brother died, a brown leaf
> against a wire fence.
> My father never got to say goodbye.
> The boy who gave his mouth to me
> saw death in a rear-view mirror,
> turned around to meet it, met it.

Because I daydreamed about how beautiful I'd be
with tears in my eyes.
Because I didn't throw myself over a grenade.
Because of my stupid fault.
How many more have I watched,
helpless, pulled over the falls?

I might have saved them,
might have torn off my senior prom gown
and dived into the torrent.

In front of my horrified eyes
they went over without a sound
like a herd of stampeding cattle
crazy with thirst.
Bloody boys, broken women,
thin children.
I might have saved them.

As dawn colors the sky
with sad gray radiance
I count the day I ran to tell Mama
we broke Jamie Crowl's arm on the seesaw,
the day I ran to tell Mama I made Jennifer
take the dangerous shortcut from school,
the day I ran to tell Mama my voodoo had worked.

I remember how she fed me Cheerios
while the news announced in a cold white voice
the numbers of the dead.
How she watched me pore over photographs
of mountains of eyeglasses, mountains of shoes,
then sent me out to play
in the twilight under the streetlamps;
how Junebugs felt heavy and horrible
under my flying feet.

I hear my baby waking up,
trying out my new name like a chant.
Before I face his wonderful eyes
I slip into my raggedy robe
and wash my hands and face.

In the mirror I look like Mama.
I lean closer and look into her eyes:
In their black pupils, I see my grandmother,

her mother, diminishing generations
of the dead, all of them Mama.

I, too, have given my child
to the murderous world.
I go to him, pick him up,
feel in my chest like warm liquid
hundreds of generations of Mama's forgiveness.

(Mama's Promises)

THE DANGEROUS CARNIVAL

One of the signs of a concussion
is dilated pupils. My son's pupils
dilate whenever he sees me.
The top of his skull
is a breastbone of paper.
I pace through the child-proofed house
and pray that he'll wake.

My life these days
is a dangerous carnival.
No wonder I pinned his blankets to him,
hid him for safekeeping
under the water of the pond.
Hungry eyes watch me walk the midway
past their rickety cages. For a dime
you can shoot at a skyful of women
in shorts and jogging shoes, or stand
at the back of the sweaty crowd
in the tent of THE FEROCIOUS BABY,
the BABY WITH VAMPIRE TEETH,
who sucked its mother's breasts so hard
she DISAPPEARED ONE NIGHT IN HER BED.

Someone recognizes me, shouts
in the pulsating rape of garish lights.
I want to run, but the baby's an anvil,
my breasts are concrete blocks,
I stagger under the weight.
In the getaway car the baby claws
at my hands; I fight to keep the wheels
on a track that bends back on itself,
its walls so steep the tires scream and scream.

I can't go on.
There's too much to do.

I can't keep up.
Somewhere behind me
someone is crying.
He's alive!
I have to take him his breast.

The blank picture windows
make this a room of trick mirrors:
as I rush to pick him up
I see a pigtailed little girl,
arms held wide for balance,
in Mama's size 10 high-heeled shoes.

(Mama's Promises)

19

BALI HAI CALLS MAMA

As I was putting away the groceries
I'd spent the morning buying
for the week's meals I'd planned
around things the baby could eat,
things my husband would eat,
and things I should eat
because they aren't too fattening,
late on a Saturday afternoon
after flinging my coat on a chair
and wiping the baby's nose
while asking my husband
what he'd fed it for lunch
and whether
the medicine I'd brought for him
had made his cough improve,
wiping the baby's nose again,
checking its diaper,
stepping over the baby
who was reeling to and from
the bottom kitchen drawer
with pots, pans, and plastic cups,
occasionally clutching the hem of my skirt
and whining to be held,
I was half listening for the phone
which never rings for me
to ring for me
and someone's voice to say that
I could forget about handing back
my students' exams which I'd had for a week,
that I was right about *The Waste Land,*
that I'd been given a raise,
all the time wondering
how my sister was doing,
whatever happened to my old lover(s),
and why my husband wanted

a certain brand of toilet paper;
and wished I hadn't, but I'd bought
another fashion magazine that promised
to make me beautiful by Christmas,
and there wasn't room for the creamed corn
and every time I opened the refrigerator door
the baby rushed to grab whatever was on the bottom shelf
which meant I constantly had to wrestle
jars of its mushy food out of its sticky hands
and I stepped on the baby's hand and the baby was screaming
and I dropped the bag of cake flour I'd bought to make cookies with
and my husband rushed in to find out what was wrong because the baby
was drowning out the sound of the touchdown although I had scooped
it up and was holding it in my arms so its crying was inside
my head like an echo in a barrel and I was running cold water
on its hand while somewhere in the back of my mind wondering what
to say about *The Waste Land* and whether I could get away with putting
broccoli in a meatloaf when

suddenly through the window
came the wild cry of geese.

(Mama's Promises)

DINOSAUR SPRING

A violet wash is streaked across the clouds.
Triceratops, Brachiosaurus, Trachodon
browse the high greenery, heave through
the dissipating mists.
They are as vacant as we are:
They don't see how mountains are growing,
how flowers change spring by spring,
how feathers form.

Last night I walked among the dinosaurs,
hardly taller than a claw.
I touched their feet with my fingertips,
my tongue numb with wonder.

At seven this morning two mallards
and a pair of Canada geese
preened themselves in the light of the pond.
Awake on a morning like this one,
jays screeching from treetop to fencepost,
I have to strain to imagine
how people wake up
in San Salvador, in Cape Town, in Beirut.
The background roar grows louder,
a neighbor screams for her child.

Just now I took my baby out of his crib
and teetered on the edge of the vortex.
I saw millions of hands imploring,
mouths open, eyes his.
I fell into a universe of black, starry water,
and through that into monstrous love
that wants to make the world right.

I can comfort my son:
The ghost in the closet, the foot-eating fish

on the floor can be washed away
with a hug and a tumbler of milk.
But the faceless face? The nuclear piñata
over our heads? The bone finger pointing?

Through the window I see the sky
that hung over the dinosaurs.
The flight of a grackle catches my eye
and pulls it down toward the moving water.
I can't see the larger motion, leaves
moldering into new soil.
If I lay on my back in the yard,
I'd feel how we're hanging on
to this planet, attached even to her
by the sheer luck of gravity.

I have to shake my head, I've grown so solemn.
It's my turn to vacuum the house.
In the din, I go back to my dream:
Holding my son by the hand,
I walk again among the dinosaurs.
In my breast my heart pours and pours
so that it terrifies me, pours and pours out
its fathomless love, like the salt mill
at the bottom of the sea.

(Mama's Promises)

23

WOMEN'S LOCKER ROOM

The splat of bare feet on wet tile
breaks the incredible luck
of my being alone in here.
I snatch a stingy towel
and sidle into the shower. I'm already soaped
by the time a white hand turns the neighboring knob.
I recognize the arm as one that flashed
for many rapid laps while I dogpaddled at the shallow end.
I dart an appraising glance: She arches down
to wash her lifted heel, and is beautiful.
As she straightens, I look into her eyes.

For an instant I remember human sacrifice:
The female explorer led skyward,
her blond tresses loose on her neck;
the drums of our pulses grew louder;
I raised the obsidian knife.
Violets bloomed in the clefts of the stairs.

I could freeze her name in an ice cube,
bottle the dirt from her footsteps
with potent graveyard dust.
I could gather the combings from her hairbrush
to burn with her fingernail clippings,
I could feed her Iago powder.
Childhood taunts, branded ears,
a thousand insults swirl through my memory
like headlines in a city vacant lot.

I jump, grimace, divide like an amoeba
into twin rages that stomp around
with their lips stuck out,
then come suddenly face to face.
They see each other and know that they
are mean mamas.

Then I bust out laughing
and let the woman live.

(Mama's Promises)

TWIST THE THREAD

Twist the thread
three times around your finger.
Pull it through.
It's so easy you forget
day winding into evening.

Spring again.
The same birds whistle
their sweet marriages,
the same trees
weave out loops
of the same new green.

End of the row.
Go back.
Begin again the rosary of yarn.

It's so easy you forget,
knitting toward night,
and you correct your life.
You think of answers
you never gave,
remember the impossible,
the failures all success.
Your fingers, touching everyone,
have learned gentleness by heart.

The friends who died come back,
their faces red
with things to tell you.
And this time you listen
with wide eyes.

No longer alone in your language
of unanswered questions,

you knit the children right,
the love for always,
the husband coming back.
Each stitch is true,
the thread taut,
the life complete in recollection,
the perfected past.

(For the Body)

FOR MARY, FOURTH MONTH

Open the drawer.
There are scissors there
like teeth in the darkness.
And, like a root,
someone is biting into
your darkness.

In your secrecy, so deep
you cannot think it out,
someone is opening hands.
O, slow and dark there,
someone is making room for hands.
Someone's legs are learning to beat
a tattoo you will not forget.
There is burrowing there,
a red light growing on the horizon,
a dim knock on your mind's door.

You shake your head.
Scissors, you say, like knives
are waiting for someone like me.
I am green, you say,
have forgotten the urgent pushings
of roots.
In the room of your body
someone is opening hands.
Someone is stretching, is dancing
to wet, secret music.
The beat, the beat of someone's feet
is teaching you new rhythms.

You awake with a start
as someone opens
sad, knowing eyes.

(For the Body)

THE MARRIAGE NIGHTMARE

He's so romantic, he's kissed both my arms
past the elbows; now he's nibbling my neck
in a motel room with pictures of kittens
on each of its dingy white walls.
He turns away to open
that odd-shaped affair on the bed,
and withdraws a tenor sax.
He plays mellow jazz as I shimmy
out of my clothes and slip between the sheets.
Then he lays it on the dresser,
pulls his sweater over his head.
The coarse black hair around his navel
leaves me breathless and oozy.
He smiles, unbuckles his belt,
and my husband bursts into the room.

I wake up to a blue day.
Downstairs, my husband and child
have already eaten breakfast.
The Sunday *Times* is scattered,
greasy, sprinkled with crumbs.
I sit in my nightgown at the table,
my head still frowsy.
My child whines against my knee;
if I concentrate hard enough
I can ignore him.
My husband demands to know
why I'm so sullen.
If I concentrate hard enough
maybe he'll go away.
The child's whining grows;
he throws the book he wants me to read.
My husband grabs him and storms out.
The door slams behind them.

I hear five smacks.
The child screams.
Then the door slams again
and my husband stands before me,
bigger than usual.
I wake up to a blue day.

(Mama's Promises)

LEVITATION WITH BABY

The Muse bumped
against my window this morning.
No one was at home but me
and the baby. The Muse said
there was room on her back for two.
Okay, I said, *but first I've got to*

Pack his favorite toys.
Small ones are the best:
that way he can sit and play quietly
as the earth slides out from under our feet.
Let's see, somewhere there's
a wind-up dog with a drum
that sometimes keeps him busy
ten minutes or more.
And we'd better take some books.

Disposable diapers,
pre-moistened towelettes,
plastic bags,
and I'll pack a lunch.
Peanut butter and crackers
are nutritious,
and the crumbs brush right off.

While I was packing his lunch
the baby got hungry,
so I put him in his high chair,
unpacked the crackers,
and gave him some.
He threw the third one down,
so I took him out,
wiped the high chair,
wiped the floor under and around the chair,
wiped the window next to it,
and wiped his fingers and face.

Then I took off his pants,
shook them out,
and wiped the soles of his shoes.

I filled two plastic bottles,
changed his diaper,
and got him dressed.
I washed my hands.
I sat down at my desk.
Okay, I said. *Now
I'm ready for takeoff.*

As he cried for a bottle,
I saw my next-door neighbor,
shirtless, in the pants he wears
to work in his garden,
scribbling furiously on the back of a paper bag
as he ascended over the roof of his house
on the Muse's huge, sun-spangled wings.

(Mama's Promises)

EMILY DICKINSON'S DEFUNCT

She used to
pack poems
in her hip pocket.
Under all the
gray old lady
clothes she was
dressed for action.
She had hair,
imagine,
in certain places, and
believe me
she smelled human
on a hot summer day.
Stalking snakes
or counting
the thousand motes
in sunlight
she walked just
like an Indian.
She was New England's
favorite daughter,
she could pray
like the devil.
She was a
two-fisted woman,
this babe.
All the flies
just stood around
and buzzed
when she died.

(For the Body)

CONFESSIONAL POEM

This friend of mine
says she'd like to visit
the lonely young mother she's seen
in a fourth floor window.
She'd climb the unswept stairs
and whisper a word,
the locks would click,
and the apartment door would open.

There, in the overheated air
and the turbulence of children,
she'd stand, the Fat Lady suit
hanging from her shoulders
like a sandwich board.

She'd strip off
the fake rabbit coat—a good buy—
and dance around in the bargain basement
housedress. She'd undo the dress snap
by snap, all the while eyeing the youngest baby
eyeing the doorway to the john.
Under the housedress she'd wear
a black nylon slip
with a side seam ripped out.

She says she'd wiggle wiggle the hips
and wink at no one in particular
as the oldest baby pulled the middle baby's hair
and the youngest disappeared through the bathroom doorway.
She'd raise the slip like an opera curtain,
ripple the cellulite thighs,
and shimmy her shoulders
to open the diaper pin
closing the back of the bra.

By now the young mother
would have left the sooty window;
she'd sit laughing on the sofa
jiggling a baby on her knees.

And my friend says she'd dance,
in the Zeppelin glory of the melony breasts,
the magnificent girth, the silver and auburn
stretch marks on the belly
like a night of Northern Lights.
She'd lift her arms and twirl like a ballerina,
then swing her elbows and tap like a dancing fool.
Heavy and beautiful, the young mother would get up
and join her, her pregnancy big
as an extra silhouette.
In the faint cloud of dust they raised
the middle baby would bend and straighten its knees,
dancing in its heavy diaper; the oldest
would throw back its head and whirl, whirl.
From the bathroom the youngest,
hearing laughter, would leave a wet trail,
then sit up and clap happy hands.

Then I'd strip off
the Fat Lady suit
and dance on, like a blaze of sunlight.

(Mama's Promises)

THE FORTUNATE SPILL

Note: Traditionally, black-eyed peas are served
on New Year's Eve: Each black-eyed pea one eats
brings luck.

Well! Johnnie thinks. *He has his nerve!*
Crashing this party! What stuck-up conceit!
Passing his induction papers around;
another Negro whose feet never touch the ground.

His name is Melvin Nelson. In his eyes
the black of dreams sparkles with laughing stars.

Johnnie agrees to play. And it defies
all explanation: she forgets five bars!
This cocky, handsome boy? she asks her heart.
For good luck all year, Melvin says, *you've got to fart.*

They eat elbow to elbow, in a crowd
of 1942's gifted black youth.
His tipsy bass-clef voice is much too loud.
Hers trebles nervously: to tell the truth,
she's impressed.

I'll be a man up in the sky,
he confides. She blurts out, *Hello, Jesus!* And they die
with laughter.

But the joke catches him off-guard:
he spills the black-eyed peas into her lap.
Oh Lord, he mumbles, but she laughs so hard
both recognize the luck of their mishap.

And I watch from this distant balcony
as they fall for each other, and for me.

(The Homeplace)

36

EPITHALAMIUM AND SHIVAREE

for Linda and Debbie

All Cana was abuzz next day with stories:
Some said it had a sad aftertaste; some said
its sweetness made them ache with thirst.
Years later those who had been there
spoke of it with closed eyes, and swayed
like the last slow-dance of the prom.
The village children poked each other's ribs
when they reeled past, still drunk at eighty.

Lovers know what that drunkenness is:
It makes a festive sacrament of praise
for the One who loans us each other
and this too-brief time.
One sip of the wine of Cana
and lovers become fools. And fools lovers.
The willows are drunk tralala; they shimmy
in the silly wind of Spring,

lovers sing noisily. With a little pink parasol
a lover pedals out to the halfway point on the wire.
Below, a silver thread of river. She waves, blows kisses,
wavers, and oops,
her unicycle disappears into mystery.
Her face mimes our gasp.
We hear an unseen, slide-whistle chorus.
She sings: *Tralala, the willows are drunk;*

they shimmy in the silly April wind.
And I'm just a kitten in catnip, a pup
rollin' in some ambrosial doggie cologne.
Why settle for less than rapture?
Your pulse against my lips, your solitude
snoring next to mine. The wine we drink from each other.
She leaps. And now there are two of them out there,
jitterbugging on shimmering air.

(Magnificat)

LIGHT UNDER THE DOOR

I remember hiding in the hall closet,
down with the dust and the extra shoes,
the hems of the big people's coats
brushing my uppermost braids. Daddy was coming.
I could tell from the crunch of wheels,
the thunk of the heavy car door,
the rattle of keys at the lock.
His hard-soled shoes came toward me,
a voice like Othello's
asked my mother where I was.
I was ready to swoon with delight,
but the footsteps faded,
the voice asked for dinner.

I remember the smell of wool,
the gritty floor under my palms,
the thin light under the door.
My mother stirred, chopped,
opened the oven to check on the cornbread.
I heard her answer my sister
while Daddy went into their bedroom
to take off his Air Force uniform.
Outside, a plane like a buzz saw
sliced the distant sky.

That day in kindergarten
a buzzer went off;
Mrs. Liebel jumped up
and made us hide on the polished floor
under our desks.
Not even the naughty boys giggled
as we watched a fly explore
the alphabet over the blackboard
and looked up at wads of petrified gum.
I'm sitting in the closet now,
waiting for the bomb.

No, that's a lie.
I'm standing here in the kitchen,
a grown-up woman, a mother,
with used breasts. Upstairs,
the man I love and our son
are playing. The baby
touches his father's knee,
steps, stops, then runs away
with his off-balance gait.
His father chases him, hooting,
to the table where they stop for breath,
then the baby squeals and takes off
for the other room.

The sun rises in the window over the breakfast table
as I scramble the eggs. Over the radio,
a pleasant male voice announces yesterday's
disasters. The jays have carried the larger crumbs off,
now they come back for the rest.

My father opened the closet door. A light like a look
into the heart of fire blinded me for a moment:
I didn't see him there.
I remember the good smell of beans and cornbread
and the clash of plates being put on the table.
I remember Mama's voice humming mezzo
as I walked out into the light.

(Mama's Promises)

I imagine driving across country
with my sister and brother.
In California we buy caps,
the kind truck drivers wear,
bright colors that keep the sun away.
We take turns at the wheel
and sing all the songs we know.
My sister's voice is like mine
and I stop singing to listen.
All night we drive through the mountains.

My brother pulls the car over
at noon in the desert
and we get out to stretch our legs.
A strange man takes our picture
standing beside the car
in our decorative skins.

In the car again
we make the other trips,
through Kansas and Oklahoma
in the pink Lincoln and the Kaiser.
We count Uncle Sam mailboxes
and white horses,
we sleep at dusk-to-dawn drive-ins.

I catch the beautiful slow smile
of our dead brother
in the rear-view mirror,
and our father in his uniform
drives 80 and when the cop stops us
—What do you think you're flying, boy?—
he answers: B-52s.

Now we are telling jokes in the farmland,
playing the dozens, getting down.

In Maine we get out to see the ocean.
We have come home again,
our old house there on the hill.

That night none of us can sleep.
In our separate rooms we lie awake
in the shared darkness
and imagine ourselves
still driving across country,
still falling home down the highway.

(For the Body)

TUSKEGEE AIRFIELD

for the Tuskegee Airmen

These men,
these proud black men:
our first to touch
their fingers to the sky.

The Germans learned to call them
Die Schwarzen Vogelmenschen.
They called themselves
The Spookwaffe.

Laughing.
And marching to class under officers
whose thin-lipped ambition
was to *wash the niggers out.*

Sitting at attention
for lectures about ailerons, airspeed, altimeters
from boring lieutenants who believed
you monkeys ain't meant to fly.

Oh, there were parties,
cadet-dances, guest appearances
by the Count
and the lovely Lena.

There was the embarrassing
adulation of Negro civilians.
A woman approached my father in a bar
where he was drinking with his buddies.
Hello, Airman. She held out her palm.
Will you tell me my future?

There was that,
like a breath of pure oxygen.
But first,
they had to earn wings.

There was this one instructor
who was pretty nice.
I mean, we just sat around
and *talked* when a flight had gone well.

But he was from Minnesota,
and he made us sing
the Minnesota Fight Song
before we took off.

If you didn't sing it,
your days were numbered.
"Minnesota, hats off to thee . . ."
That bastard!

One time I had a check-flight
with an instructor from Louisiana.
As we were about to head for base,
he chopped the power.

Forced landing, nigger.
There were trees everywhere I looked.
Except on that little island . . .
I began my approach.

The instructor said, *Pull up.*
That was an excellent approach.
Real surprised.
But where would you have taken off, wise guy?

I said, *Sir,*
I was ordered
to land the plane.
Not take off.

The instructor grinned.
Boy, if your ass
is as hard as your head,
you'll go far in this world.

(The Homeplace)

FREEMAN FIELD

for Edward Wilson Woodward, Captain USAF (ret.)
and the 101 of the 477th

It was a cool evening
in the middle of April.
The 477th, the only Negro
bombardier group in the Air Corps,
had just been transferred
to Freeman Field.

Some of the guys
said they were hungry
and left to find food.
The others went on
playing bridge,
mending socks,
writing letters home.

A few minutes later
the hungry guys came back,
still hungry.
We're under arrest.

The others thought they were kidding.

The next morning
the Base Commander
issued new regulations:
Negro officers were assigned
to the NCO Club;
white officers were assigned
to the Officers' Club.

The Base Commander,
who had deliberately busted
an entire Negro outfit
so he wouldn't have to be

their flight-leader in combat,
was a graduate of West Point.

He issued a statement:
If we do not allow
Negro and white officers to mix,
the accident rate
will go down two
and two-tenths
percent.

Sixty-one Negro officers
were ordered to report
one by one
to his office.
Lieutenant, have you read the regulations?
Sign here if you have read and understood.

Sixty-one Negro officers
refused to sign.
A man of your intelligence
must be able to recognize
the dangers of fraternization.

They refused to sign.
This is an order:
Sign the document.

They refused to sign.
This is a direct order!
You will sign the document!

Six cargo planes were called in;
pilots, navigators, and bombardiers
were shoved on board and flown
to Godman Field, Kentucky.

Across the river
was Fort Knox.
The sixty-one
had grown by now
to one hundred and one
American fliers trained
to fight Nazis.
They were confined
to the BOQ
under guard
of armed MPs.

By night, searchlights watched
every window. By daylight
the men leaned in the windows
to smoke, watching
the German POWs pump gas,
wash windshields
and laugh
at the motorpool
across the street.

(The Homeplace)

LONELY EAGLES

for Daniel "Chappie" James, General USAF
and for the 332d Fighter Group

Being black in America
was the Original Catch,
so no one was surprised
by 22:
The segregated airstrips,
separate camps.
They did the jobs
they'd been trained to do.

Black ground crews kept them in the air;
black flight surgeons kept them alive;
the whole Group removed their headgear
when another pilot died.

They were known by their names:
"Ace" and "Lucky,"
"Sky-hawk Johnny," "Mr. Death."
And by their positions and planes.
Red Leader to Yellow Wing-man,
do you copy?

If you could find a fresh egg
you bought it and hid it
in your dopp-kit or your boot
until you could eat it alone.
On the night before a mission
you gave a buddy
your hiding-places
as solemnly
as a man dictating
his will.
There's a chocolate bar
in my Bible;

my whiskey bottle
is inside my bedroll.

In beat-up Flying Tigers
that had seen action in Burma,
they shot down three German jets.
They were the only outfit
in the American Air Corps
to sink a destroyer
with fighter planes.
Fighter planes with names
like "By Request."
Sometimes the radios
didn't even work.

They called themselves
"Hell from Heaven."
This Spookwaffe.
My father's old friends.

It was always
maximum effort:
A whole squadron
of brother-men
raced across the tarmac
and mounted their planes.

    My tent-mate was a guy named Starks.
    The funny thing about me and Starks
    was that my air mattress leaked,
    and Starks' didn't.
    Every time we went up,

I gave my mattress to Starks
and put his on my cot.

One day we were strafing a train.
Strafing's bad news:
you have to fly so low and slow
you're a pretty clear target.
My other wing-man and I
exhausted our ammunition and got out.
I recognized Starks
by his red tail
and his rudder's trim-tabs.
He couldn't pull up his nose.
He dived into the train
and bought the farm.

I found his chocolate,
three eggs, and a full fifth
of his hoarded-up whiskey.
I used his mattress
for the rest of my tour.

It still bothers me, sometimes:
I was sleeping
on his breath.

(The Homeplace)

50

STAR-FIX

for Melvin M. Nelson, Captain USAF (ret.) (1917–1966)

At his cramped desk
under the astrodome,
the navigator looks
thousands of light-years
everywhere but down.
He gets a celestial fix,
measuring head winds;
checking the log;
plotting wind-speed,
altitude, drift
in a circle of protractors,
slide-rules, and pencils.

He charts in his Howgozit
the points of no alternate
and of no return.
He keeps his eyes on the compass,
the two altimeters, the map.
He thinks, *Do we have enough fuel?*
What if my radio fails?

He's the only Negro in the crew.
The only black flier on the whole base,
for that matter. Not that it does:
this crew is a team.
Bob and Al, Les, Smitty, Nelson.

Smitty, who said once
after a poker game,
I love you, Nelson.
I never thought I could love
a colored man.
When we get out of this man's Air Force,
if you ever come down to Tuscaloosa,

look me up and come to dinner.
You can come in the front door, too;
hell, you can stay overnight!
Of course, as soon as you leave,
I'll have to burn down my house.
Because if I don't
my neighbors will.

The navigator knows where he is
because he knows where he's been
and where he's going.
At night, since he can't fly
by dead-reckoning,
he calculates his position
by shooting a star.

The octant tells him
the angle of a fixed star
over the artificial horizon.
His position in that angle
is absolute and true:
Where the hell are we, Nelson?
Alioth, in the Big Dipper.
Regulus. Antares, in Scorpio.

He plots their lines
of position on the chart,
gets his radio bearing,
corrects for lost time.

Bob, Al, Les, and Smitty
are counting on their navigator.
If he sleeps,
they all sleep.

If he fails,
they fall.

The navigator keeps watch
over the night and the instruments,
going hungry for five or six hours
to give his flight-lunch
to his two little girls.

(The Homeplace)

PORTER

for Bertram Wilson, Lieutenant Colonel USAF (ret.)
and for all of my "uncles"

Suddenly
when I hear airplanes overhead—
big, silver ones
whose muscles fill the sky—
I listen: That sounds like
someone I know.
And the sky
looks much closer.

I know my intimacy, now,
with the wheel and roar
of wind around wings.
Hello, wind.
Take care of my people.
The moon and stars
aren't so white now;
some of my people
know their first names.
Hey, Arcturus.
What's happening, Polaris?
Daddy said I should look you up.

You're even
more
dumbfounding
than he told me you were.

This is my other heritage:
I have roots in the sky.
The Tuskegee Airmen
are my second family.
This new, brave,
decorated tribe.

My family.
My homeplace, at last.
It was there
all through time.
I only had
to raise my eyes.

Tuskegee Airmen,
uncles of my childhood,
how shall I live and work
to match your goodness?
Can I do more
than murmur name upon name,
as the daughter
of a thousand proud fathers?

Jefferson.
Wilson.
Sparks.
Toliver.
Woodward.
Mitchell.
Price.
Lacy.
Straker.
Smith.
Washington.
Meriweather.
White . . .

    One time, this was in the Sixties,
    and I was a full-bird Colonel,
    they called me in Kentucky

and asked me to pick up
an aircraft somebody had crashed
down in Louisiana.
I was supposed to fly it
to a base in New Mexico
and go back to Kentucky
on a commercial flight.

It's tricky business,
flying a plane that's been crashed.
You can never tell
what might still be wrong with it.

Okay, I flew the plane to New Mexico
and got on a flight back home.
I was in full dress uniform,
decorations and medals
and shit
all over my chest.
The Distinguished Flying Cross
with two Bronze Oak Leaf Clusters,
The Bronze Star,
a couple of commendation medals,
a European-African-Middle East Campaign Medal
with four Bronze Service Stars . . .

When we landed in Chicago
I was standing in the aisle
when a lady—
a little grayhaired white lady—
asked me to lift
her suitcase down.
I said, *Of course,*
and carried it on out
into the terminal for her.

When I put it down
she handed me a dime
as a tip.

He looks down.
Then he looks at me and grins.

I TOOK it, too!

(The Homeplace)

RECURRENT DREAM

My father came back regularly, to see
how I was doing, long after he died.
He came in dreams in which he lovingly
explained that he'd returned to be my guide
through the important shadows. I awoke
and all day saw day's light intensified.
The last time, in an aureole of smoke
that somehow shone, he stood outside my door.
I didn't open it. Instead, I spoke:
"I'm grown up. I don't need you anymore."
He smiled and nodded, saying, "Yes, I know."
Last night I had another visitor:
Love's ghost, as though compelled by need, as though
it knew the way. My love, I'm grown. Let go.

(Partial Truth)

THE DREAM'S WISDOM

I dreamed
Mama came back
for a borrowed day.
We knew she would die again;
her heart was irrevocably set.
She was so dear to me.
I knew
a new
gentleness.

Help me greet everyone I know
with the dream's
wisdom.

(Magnificat)

II

HOMEPLACE

CHURCHGOING

after Philip Larkin

The Lutherans sit stolidly in rows;
only their children feel the holy ghost
that makes them jerk and bobble and almost
destroys the pious atmosphere for those
whose reverence bows their backs as if in work.
The congregation sits, or stands to sing,
or chants the dusty creeds automaton.
Their voices drone like engines, on and on,
and they remain untouched by everything;
confession, praise, or likewise, giving thanks.
The organ that they saved years to afford
repeats the Sunday rhythms song by song,
slow lips recite the credo, smother yawns,
and ask forgiveness for being so bored.

I, too, am wavering on the edge of sleep,
and ask myself again why I have come
to probe the ruins of this dying cult.
I come bearing the cancer of my doubt
as superstitious suffering women come
to touch the magic hem of a saint's robe.

Yet this has served two centuries of men
as more than superstitious cant; they died
believing simply. Women, satisfied
that this was truth, were racked and burned with them
for empty words we moderns merely chant.

We sing a spiritual as the last song,
and we are moved by a peculiar grace
that settles a new aura on the place.
This simple melody, though sung all wrong,
captures exactly what I think is faith.
Were you there when they crucified my Lord?

That slaves should suffer in his agony!
That Christian, slave-owning hypocrisy
nevertheless was by these slaves ignored
as they pitied the poor body of Christ!
Oh, sometimes it causes me to tremble,
that they believe most, who so much have lost.
To be a Christian one must bear a cross.
I think belief is given to the simple
as recompense for what they do not know.

I sit alone, tormented in my heart
by fighting angels, one group black, one white.
The victory is uncertain, but tonight
I'll lie awake again, and try to start
finding the black way back to what we've lost.

(For the Body)

MY GRANDFATHER WALKS IN THE WOODS

Somewhere
in the light above the womb,
black trees
and white trees
populate a world.

It is a March landscape,
the only birds around are small
and black.
What do they eat,
sitting in the birches
like warnings?

The branches of the trees
are black and white.
Their race is winter.
They thrive in cold.

There is my grandfather
walking among the trees.
He does not notice
his fingers are cold.
His black felt hat
covers his eyes.

He is knocking on each tree,
listening to their voices
as they answer slowly
deep, deep from their roots.
I am John, he says,
are you my father?

They answer
with voices like wind
blowing away from him.

(For the Body)

HOW I DISCOVERED POETRY

It was like soul-kissing, the way the words
filled my mouth as Mrs. Purdy read from her desk.
All the other kids zoned an hour ahead to 3:15,
but Mrs. Purdy and I wandered lonely as clouds borne
by a breeze off Mount Parnassus. She must have seen
the darkest eyes in the room brim: The next day
she gave me a poem she'd chosen especially for me
to read to the all except for me white class.
She smiled when she told me to read it, smiled harder,
said oh yes I could. She smiled harder and harder
until I stood and opened my mouth to banjo playing
darkies, pickaninnies, disses and dats. When I finished
my classmates stared at the floor. We walked silent
to the buses, awed by the power of words.

I AM YOU AGAIN

I am you again
as you walk through the corridor.
The ceiling is as high as heaven
and echoes your tapping feet on the waxed floor.
Nobody stares at you yet,
a small black child too awkward to play ball.

You stop at Mrs. Purdy's door.
It opens.
Five rows of blue and green eyes
like the marbles you won last summer
that you keep in the old fishbowl.
Five times six faces
under hair like straw, like silk,
like the mule's tail
if the mule's tail were table brown
or dry-grass brown
or brown as orange pop with coke.

The faces like empty sheets of pale paper
watching you,
waiting to see you jig
or wet your pants
or marry someone's sister.

You go in
and I go in with you.
We sit all year alone
on one side of the room
and learn only years later
how loudly we can say our names.

(For the Body)

SISTERS

The school bus drove us home from high school, where
we got off in the Negro neighborhood
and several times a week there was a fight:
one sister called another sister "hoe,"
pulled out black handfuls of her straightened hair,
clawed at her face and hands, and ripped her shirt.
I walked home. I believed in sisterhood.
I still do, after thirty years, although
I'll never understand why several white
sisters walked on me as if I was dirt.
We were all sisters, feminists, I thought,
forgetting what those catfights should have taught.
I was too well brought-up, too middle class
to call a heifer out, and whup her ass.

(Partial Truth)

IT'S ALL IN YOUR HEAD

for Deborah M.

How easily my heart falls back into habits:
a little stress, and I'm checking my pulse again
for irregular beats.
Just last year I went once a week
to the emergency room,
afraid my breath would expand
the radiant pain in my chest.
I lay among the hurt, the dying,
checking my symptoms off on a mental list.

I didn't die; I napped
on the spotless stainless steel beds.
I went home chastened, humble,
to the steeplechase of my life.
Now, like a bass drum dropped down the stairs,
my heart wakes me up again at night.
I pretend I'm not afraid
as the funeral procession
comes to order under my ribs.

I wanted to twirl a baton
in the 2085 parade.
The day Mrs. Gray said I'd be famous,
the sixth grade class dissolved
to an image of high-stepping white boots.
But now I stumble after, out of step,
as the band strikes up a hymn
and the colored congregation
slowly begins to move.

The trombone fades in the distance
with the flattened-out trumpets and drums;
my ancestors carry black parasols:
Diverne, Annie, Ray, Mary, Charlie.

Geneva, Oneida, Zilphia, Blanche,
in shabby shoes and black straw hats
rescued from the backs of their closets.
Dark dresses reserved for such occasions
flicker around their calves.

Their felt fedoras in their hands,
their collars too white,
their heads small
with new haircuts, my grandfathers
and uncles walk in the bright morning.
Pete has taken off his apron,
John, his overalls. Melvin, Rufus, Pomp,
in shiny shoes and suits, march
with Mister Tyler and the women.

I limp behind in my black hole shoes,
my hair crocheted with tangles
as it was when I was ten.
My old heart groans
when the brass light from the tuba
takes the road that winds up the hill.
I hear the sisters ahead of me
join in a church-house moan
as the band ascends into the blues.

The moan changes
to a melody vaguely familiar,
though they're too far away now
for me to hear more than snatches.
I hum along with them,
halting and out of sync,
like a jay
in a tree full of finches.

It's jazz I hear now from the heights,
hands clap a rhythm like approaching rain.
I want to be a part of that music,
but I fall back again and again,
damned impossible stone.
By the time I pant up the narrow ridge
only the thin voice of a clarinet
rises from small blacks and lights.

It's too soon for me to follow them over
from the top of my birth date
to the other side of the dash,
where I'll be welcomed with fanfare.
This syncopation's only a habit
my heart has picked up.
So I march back home
to the business
of putting on diapers
and taking them off.

(Mama's Promises)

THE CENTURY QUILT

for Sarah Mary Taylor, Quilter

My sister and I were in love
with Meema's Indian blanket.
We fell asleep under army green
issued to Daddy by Supply.
When Meema came to live with us
she brought her medicines, her cane,
and the blanket I found on my sister's bed
the last time I visited her.
I remembered how I'd planned to inherit
that blanket, how we used to wrap ourselves
at play in its folds and be chieftains
and princesses.

Now I've found a quilt
I'd like to die under;
Six Van Dyke brown squares,
two white ones, and one square
the yellowbrown of Mama's cheeks.
Each square holds a sweet gum leaf
whose fingers I imagine
would caress me into the silence.

I think I'd have good dreams
for a hundred years under this quilt,
as Meema must have, under her blanket,
dreamed she was a girl again in Kentucky
among her yellow sisters,
their grandfather's white family
nodding at them when they met.
When their father came home from his store
they cranked up the pianola
and all of the beautiful sisters
giggled and danced.
She must have dreamed about Mama

when the dancing was over:
a lanky girl trailing after her father
through his Oklahoma field.

Perhaps under this quilt
I'd dream of myself,
of my childhood of miracles,
of my father's burnt umber pride,
my mother's ochre gentleness.
Within the dream of myself
perhaps I'd meet my son
or my other child, as yet unconceived.
I'd call it the Century Quilt,
after its pattern of leaves.

(Mama's Promises)

I SEND MAMA HOME

I send you down the road from Paden
scaring bobwhites and pheasants
back into the weeds;
a jackrabbit keeps pace
in front of your headlights
if you drive there at night.
I send you to Boley
past a stand of post oaks
and the rolling blackjack hills.

On Pecan Street
a brown rectangle outlines the spot
where King's Ice House used to be.
The Farmer's and Merchant's Bank
is closed, grizzled boards
blind its windows.
The ghosts of Mister Turner,
the murdered banker,
and Floyd Birdwell,
the right hand of Pretty Boy Floyd,
spill like shadows
over the splintering floor.

This was the city of promise,
the town where no white man
showed his face after dark.
The *Progress* extolled it
in twice weekly headlines
as "Boley, the Negro's Dream."

Mama, I give you this poem
so you can drive past
Hazel's Department Store,
Bragg's Barber Shop,
the Truelove Cafe,

the Antioch Baptist Church,
the C.M.E. church and school,
the Creek-Seminole college.

I deliver you again
to your parents' bedroom
where the piano gleamed
like a black pegasus,
to the three-room farmhouse,
to the Oklahoma plains.
I give you the horses, Prince and Lady,
and the mules. I give you your father's car,
a Whippet, which you learned to drive
at a slow bounce through the pasture.
I give you the cows and calves
you and your brother played rodeo on,
the full smokehouse, the garden,
the fields of peanuts and cotton.

I send you back
to the black town you missed
when you were at college
and on the great white way.
I let you see
behind the mask you've worn
since the fifty-year-ago morning
when you waved goodbye from the train.

(Mama's Promises)

THE HOUSE ON MOSCOW STREET

It's the ragged source of memory,
a tarpaper-shingled bungalow
whose floors tilt toward the porch,
whose back yard ends abruptly
in a weedy ravine. Nothing special:
a chain of three bedrooms
and a long side porch turned parlor
where my great-grandfather, Pomp, smoked
every evening over the news,
a long sunny kitchen
where Annie, his wife,
measured cornmeal,
dreaming through the window
across the ravine and up to Shelby Hill
where she had borne their spirited,
high-yellow brood.

In the middle bedroom's hard,
high antique double bed,
the ghost of Aunt Jane,
the laundress
who bought the house in 1872,
though I call with all my voices,
does not appear.
Nor does Pomp's ghost,
with whom one of my cousins believes
she once had a long and intimate
unspoken midnight talk.
He told her, though they'd never met,
that he loved her; promised
her raw widowhood would heal
without leaving a scar.

The conveniences in an enclosed corner
of the slant-floored back side porch

were the first indoor plumbing in town.
Aunt Jane put them in,
incurring the wrath of the woman
who lived in the big house next door.
Aunt Jane left the house
to Annie, whose mother she had known
as a slave on the plantation,
so Annie and Pomp could move their children
into town, down off Shelby Hill.
My grandmother, her brother, and five sisters
watched their faces change slowly
in the oval mirror on the wall outside the door
into teachers' faces, golden with respect.
Here Geneva, the randy sister,
damned their colleges,
daubing her quicksilver breasts
with gifts of perfume.

As much as love,
as much as a visit
to the grave of a known ancestor,
the homeplace moves me not to silence
but to righteous, praise Jesus song:

Oh, catfish and turnip greens,
hot-water cornbread and grits.
Oh, musty, much-underlined Bibles;
generations lost to be found,
to be found.

(The Homeplace)

The house of myth;
the house that shame built;
the house given to Diverne.
The myth of a slave woman
who had to be broken, but bore
two children, neither Negro
nor white. The myth
of their father.

The myth of She Loved Him,
She Loved Herself Not.

Three generations removed
from the finest house on Shelby Hill,
my cousin and I pray for a will,
a manumission paper, a deed,
turning crumbling pages
in a dark room
in the dim county courthouse.

We find names:
Die Viernan.
Die Hammock.
Diverna Matson.
Diverne Atwood.
And from them we decipher
the faint history
of a woman nineteen years a slave.

Her first child was born
three years before freedom,
her second on the threshold
of the Great Jubilation.
She married Alf Hammock
("black," the papers state),

when her first child was nine;
Alf divorced her ten years later.
She'd apparently taken up
with Val Matson, a blacksmith ("black"),
whom she married in 1888.
That same year Val Matson willed
his house to Diverne,
adding a few months later
a bitter codicil
leaving his house to his son,
and Diverne an inheritance
of five
measly dollars.

Nigger, I got me a house
already and two bright-skin childrens,
I don't need your promises nor
your black backside neither,
I had me a man in my life,
can't no mangy halfman scrounge
around up under my skirts, you
can do your own
damn cooking.

Diverne's house
was queen of Shelby Hill.
Where it once stood, we found
a car seat and a lot of used condoms.

(The Homeplace)

TO MARKET

All the long way from Jamaica
in the nightmare
the old folks always told you
would carry you off someday,
you stank of boat-sickness,
your first woman-blood
doubling you over with cramps,
but you hustled anyway
when they told you to,
then teetered, blinded by sunshine,
praise Jesus on dry land again.

From New Orleans you were part of a shipment
of twenty-four new and used slaves.
You heard them call Natchez,
Vicksburg, Rosedale, Memphis, Blytheville,
Dyersburg, Hickman.
With each strange name you lost
two or three holdmates.
The last name you heard
was Columbus, Kentucky.

Given a week to rest,
you washed and replaited your hair,
hemmed the dress
the dealer had thrown
in your lap.
You were three together
in the holding house;
they whispered terrible tales:
Bastard's woman love me better,
the reason Master sold me
away from home.
Master catched me
when I run away north:

the son of the devil
thought he could whip me.
Sold me, instead.

One morning before dawn,
the dealer announced
your next stop: Clinton.
Twelve dusty miles
you marched barefoot,
one ankle raw from the chain.
The dealer rode in front,
high on his broad-backed brown horse,
whistling quietly.
Children ran to see you up close
through splintery split-rail fences;
men and women chopping cotton
straightened up to watch you walk past.

(The Homeplace)

Diverne stands in the kitchen as they dance,
laughing and flirting, on the bare parlor floor.
She's taken up the rug, glad for the chance,
at last, to beat it free of sins outdoors.

Her fancy cakes are popular, her punch
has earned light giggles from Miss Atwood's friends.
She'd struggled at Miss Atwood's back to cinch
that tiny waist. *Miss Atwood look right grand.*

Mister Tyler asks for a water-glass of rye:
he's just enlisted, a drop-out from law school.
She notices something dangerous in his eye:
Crazy damn white man, acting like a fool.

Taking her hands, Henry Tyler gives her a twirl
and off they waltz. He swirls Diverne so fast
her head kerchief unknots itself. He smiles
down at Diverne's embarrassment, and gasps:

They blush! Hearing the whispers from the walls,
he sees men grin. His father shakes his head.
But *(That dark rose . . .)* he dances. *What the hell,
who knows, next week, next month, I could be dead.*

(The Homeplace)

BALANCE

He watch her like a coonhound watch a tree.
What might explain the metamorphosis
he underwent when she paraded by
with tea-cakes, in her fresh and shabby dress?
(As one would carry water from a well—
straight-backed, high-headed, like a diadem,
with careful grace so that no drop will spill—
she balanced, almost brimming, her one name.)

She think she something, stuck-up island bitch.
Chopping wood, hanging laundry on the line,
and tantalizingly within his reach,
she honed his body's yearning to a keen,
sharp point. And on that point she balanced life.
That hoe Diverne think she Marse Tyler's wife.

(The Homeplace)

83

CHOSEN

Diverne wanted to die, that August night
his face hung over hers, a sweating moon.
She wished so hard, she killed part of her heart.

If she had died, her one begotten son,
her life's one light, would never have been born.
Pomp Atwood might have been another man:

born with a single race, another name.
Diverne might not have known the starburst joy
her son would give her. And the man who came

out of a twelve-room house and ran to her
close shack across three yards that night, to leap
onto her cornshuck pallet. Pomp was their

share of the future. And it wasn't rape.
In spite of her raw terror. And his whip.

(The Homeplace)

DAUGHTERS, 1900

Five daughters, in the slant light on the porch,
are bickering. The eldest has come home
with new truths she can hardly wait to teach.

She lectures them: the younger daughters search
the sky, elbow each other's ribs, and groan.
Five daughters, in the slant light on the porch

and blue-sprigged dresses, like a stand of birch
saplings whose leaves are going yellow-brown
with new truths. They can hardly wait to teach,

themselves, to be called "Ma'am," to march
high-heeled across the hanging bridge to town.
Five daughters. In the slant light on the porch

Pomp lowers his paper for a while, to watch
the beauties he's begotten with his Ann:
these new truths they can hardly wait to teach.

The eldest sniffs, "A lady doesn't scratch."
The third snorts back, "Knock, knock: nobody home."
The fourth concedes, "Well, maybe not in *church* . . ."
Five daughters in the slant light on the porch.

(The Homeplace)

CHOPIN

It's Sunday evening. Pomp holds the receipts
of all the colored families on the Hill
in his wide lap, and shows which white store cheats
these patrons, who can't read a weekly bill.
His parlor's full of men holding their hats
and women who admire his girls' good hair.
Pomp warns them not to trust the Democrats,
controlling half of Hickman from his chair.
The varying degrees of cheating seen,
he nods toward the piano. Slender, tall,
a Fisk girl passing-white, almost nineteen,
his Blanche folds the piano's paisley shawl
and plays Chopin. And blessed are the meek
who have to buy in white men's stores next week.

(The Homeplace)

HURRAH, HURRAH

A full moon rises
over perfect weather
on a hillside in France.
Surrounded by soft laughter
about men who wear their gas masks
in the open latrine,
Sgt. Atwood checks the wires.
As the Allies push toward Metz
the 325th is encamped in Pont-à-Mousson.
Atwood's in charge of the switchboard
and the lives of his men.

The night explodes
with noise first,
then with light.
One shell has destroyed
generals' communications;
the other, unexploded,
scatters the men into panic.
Only the dead
and Sgt. Atwood
remain at their posts.

Atwood spends three hours
connecting and reconnecting the lines.
Reconnecting because more German shells,
like jealous overseers,
keep undoing his work.

When the ammunitions dump
two blocks away takes a direct hit,
Atwood's knocked off his feet.
But the lines are restored.

The front page of the *Courier*
brings the news home:
LOCAL BOY ARMY HERO.
Pomp's fingers soften the clipping
to blurred words on white velvet,
showing it around town.
MY BOY GOT THE BRONZE STAR.

He sits several hours
in the moonlight one evening,
then writes:

        Take your bonus money
        and buy a dark suit
        to come home in.
        Chief Wright's meeting the trains.
        Keep your uniform in the suitcase.

When Rufus comes
they close the curtains
and lock the doors
before seeing, for the first time,
their son and brother in full glory.

Three days later
a colored soldier
is lynched on Main Street.

Rufus never wears the uniform
again in his life.
A black man in France
wasn't the same
as a black man at home.

(The Homeplace)

THE BALLAD OF AUNT GENEVA

Geneva was the wild one.
Geneva was a tart.
Geneva met a blue-eyed boy
and gave away her heart.

Geneva ran a roadhouse.
Geneva wasn't sent
to college like the others:
Pomp's pride her punishment.

She cooked out on the river,
watching the shore slide by,
her lips pursed into hardness,
her deep-set brown eyes dry.

They say she killed a woman
over a good black man
by braining the jealous heifer
with an iron frying pan.

They say, when she was eighty,
she got up late at night
and sneaked her old, white lover in
to make love, and to fight.

First, they heard the tell-tale
singing of the springs,
then Geneva's voice rang out:
I need to buy some things,

So next time, bring more money.
And bring more moxie, too.
I ain't got no time to waste
on limp white mens like you.

Oh yeah? Well, Mister White Man,
it sure might be stone-white,
but my thing's white as it is.
And you know damn well I'm right.

Now listen: take your heart pills
and pay the doctor mind.
If you up and die on me,
I'll whip your white behind.

They tiptoed through the parlor
on heavy, time-slowed feet.
She watched him, from her front door,
walk down the dawnlit street.

Geneva was the wild one.
Geneva was a tart.
Geneva met a blue-eyed boy
and gave away her heart.

(The Homeplace)

HIGH AND HAUGHTY

Ray, almost a spinster, gave up
her dreams of princes to marry
a widowed farmer she'd refused
as a proud, lanky girl.
He was intelligent, kind.
And who would be good enough?

On her husband's farm
near Boley, Oklahoma,
she was surprised by love,
like a rainbow umbrella
unfolding over their heads.

New people arrived every week,
having heard of an all-black town
from an incredulous mouth
or a Negro newspaper.
Having heard of her husband.
See that big tree?
If you talk to the man that lives there
he'll loan you enough to get by,
maybe lend you a mule.

They weren't rich,
but John would give away
the drawers on his behind
if Ray didn't stop him.
John, think of the children . . .

She loved John
not because he'd made her
his wife and the mother of two
when she was well past thirty.

She loved John because
early one July evening,

after stopping his car in the road,
wading through a peanut field,
taking off his hat
and handkerchiefing his forehead,
a white man called toward the house:
Mister Mitchell?

And Ray became,
at long last,
a queen.

(The Homeplace)

JUNETEENTH

With her shiny black-patent sandals
and her Japanese parasol,
and wearing a brand-new Juneteenth dress,
Johnnie's a living doll.

Juneteenth: when the Negro telegraph
reached the last sad slave . . .

It's Boley's second Easter;
the whole town a picnic.
Children run from one church booth
to the next, buying sandwiches,
sweet-potato pie, peach cobbler
with warm, sweaty pennies.

The flame of celebration
ripples like glad news
from one mouth to the next.

These people slipped away
in the middle of the night;
arrived in Boley with nothing
but the rags on their backs.
These carpenters, contractors, cobblers.
These bankers and telephone operators.
These teachers, preachers, and clerks.
These merchants and restauranteurs.
These peanut-growing farmers,
these wives halting the advance of cotton
with flowers in front of their homes.

Johnnie's father tugs one of her plaits,
head-shaking over politics
with the newspaper editor,
who lost his other ear
getting away from a lynch mob.

(The Homeplace)

ARMED MEN

Ray teaches at the Boley Baptist School,
a little too far away
to travel safely there and back
by buggy every day.
Some years she lets the children stay
on the farm with their doting father,
but this year they're toeing the line at school,
although keeping them here is a bother.

She has to watch them all the time:
Boley's a Negro town,
and sometimes carloads of white men
drive through, looking around.

Today, for instance, as she'd held
silk yard-goods to her cheek
and smiled at the extravagance,
she'd heard the screen door creak,
and a young, fair-haired white man
had stalked in. His dismissing eyes
had registered Mr. Oliver's store:
first contemptuous, then surprised.

Mr. Oliver said, *Good morning, Sir,*
one moment please. Miss Ray,
you look Easter-fine this morning.
Can I cut that silk today?

The white man spat a bad name;
Mr. Oliver prepared to fight.
The white man promised to bring some friends
and shoot up the town tonight.

And now, Ray's children expect her
to let them go out and run
through the twilit streets of Boley,
where each window holds a loaded gun.

(The Homeplace)

AUNT ANNIE'S PRAYER

Luke 2:36–37

Her magnified voice reverberates
from the white-splashed red brick walls.
The congregation fanning itself
in sticky mahogany pews
nods, amens, and thanks the Lord.
Above her head and the altar
a hand-painted diptych offers
two alternatives: the blond Jesus
yearning heavenward in Gethsemane;
the dark-eyed Good Shepherd
cradling newborn white lambs.
The junior choir stirs
in its loft on the right;
on the left the senior choir
hums and sways in response.

Praise Jesus. We are here
together again this Sunday.
He bore us through the floods last week;
He kept us dry
in the high place at His side.
He woke us up
to glad daylight this morning;
He cast rays of His pure joy
over our problems and pains.

Still, we don't thank Him
as much as we should.
He brought us through,
and still we don't thank Him.
He fed our souls,
and still we don't thank Him.
He gave us children,
and still we don't thank Him.
He made us new music,

and still we don't thank Him.
He lifted us up,
and still we don't thank Him.
He gave us our dignity,
and still we don't thank Him.
He gave us salvation,
and still we don't thank Him.
He bought our freedom,
and still we don't thank Him.
Lord, he set us free,
and still we don't thank Him.

Father in heaven,
I thank You this morning.
I thank You that You have given us
this hallowed day.
I thank You that You have made us
into this nation of fellowship,
conceived in slavery's deceit
but raised on the breast-milk of truth.

We need You, Lord.
Lend us Your stone strength.
For the burden is heavy
and the highway is steep.
Yes, Lord, sometimes it seem like
we're almost there, almost there,
and the stone rumbles on back down.
So many thousand gone.
Yes, Lord, we need You now
more than ever before.

As You shared our enslavement, Lord,
through your son, Jesus:
when we were heartdead;

when we were woe-begotten, bleeding and whipped:
Be with us again.

I've seen through the cloud,
brothers and sisters;
yes,
I've seen through the cloud
to His welcoming face.

       See through the cloud . . .

Yes, Lord, I've seen
the promise of life.
Let us stand and join our choir
in praise. Thank You, Jesus.

       See through the cloud . . .

I've seen through the cloud.

       . . . into the rapture
       that shines from His face.
       See, by His light,
       His beautiful light,
       our covenant:
       justice and grace.

Praise God.
Thank You, Jesus.
Amen.
Amen.

       (The Homeplace)

THUS FAR BY FAITH

Thomas Chapel C.M.E., Hickman, Kentucky

I Sermon in the Cotton Field
Philippians 2:12b–15a

His heart's upwelling of its own accord
slackens the reins, stopping the plow mid-row
beside a sea of furrows, as the word
whirling within takes shape: *Whoa, brothers, whoa.*
One mule cranes questioningly; the other nips
his neck, ears back. They bray against the hitch
which matches them. And Uncle Warren wraps
his arms around the sky and starts to preach.

Beloved, stop your grumbling. Be the stars
what give a twisted generation light.
That's what the book say. But old Satan roars
louder, sometimes, than Master. He say, Hate
the whip-hand and the yoke: Why be a fool?
The Lord Hisself were tempted, Brother Mule.

II Sermon in the Woodlot
1 Corinthians 9:24–27

The Lord Himself was tested, Brother Mule,
but y'all would try the patience of a saint.
There's only a few more loads of lumber to haul;
Git up, there! You know Master don't know no cain't.
The Book say, Run so as to win the crown
imperishable. That mean man must grunt
and sweat from first light til the sun sink down,
same as a mule. We can run lightfoot with praise
or toting a croaker sack of dead-weight sins around.
Come on now, git.
                        The wagon creaks and sways,
a mockingbird trills from a branch almost overhead.

Uncle Warren nods to a quietly working slave
whose bare brown back is criss-crossed with black and red.
The mules meander into sunshine, leaving the wood.

III Sermon in the Ruined Garden
James 2:14–18

A mule meanders into sunshine from the wood
near Sally's garden. Almost nothing left
after the locust tides of the bereft
swept north. Some die for truth; some died for food.
Uncle Warren plucks a few choice stalks of grass,
chirrups and holds it in an outstretched hand.
The mule flinches just out of reach, to stand
flat-eared, tail flickering, willful as an ass.
Uncle Warren says, *Uh-huh: You think you smart.*
Well, don't hee-haw to me about how faith
helped you survive the deluge. Save your breath.
Show me. Faith without works ain't worth a fart.
People is hungry. Act out your faith now
by hitching your thanks for God's love to my plow.

IV Meditation over the Washtub
Exodus 19:4–6a

Oh, I'm hitching my love for Jesus to my plow;
Aunt Sally hums thanksgiving to her Lord,
pausing occasionally to wipe her brow,
scrubbing wet, soapy darks on the washboard.
The clean whites undulate against a breeze
scented with hyacinth and simmering greens.
So this is freedom: the peace of hours like these,
and wages, now, for every house she cleans.
Her singing starts as silence, then her throat
fills with a bubble of expanding praise.

A deeper silence underlies each note:
a lifting mystery, the sky of grace.
Aunt Sally sings, *Yes, Jesus is my friend.*
Hosannas rise like incense on the wind.

V Palm Sunday, 1866
1 Peter 2:22–24

Make our hosannas incense on the wind;
may we wave palms of welcome . . . Listening
from the colored pew, Aunt Sally nods amen.
From beside her, T.T., bored and fidgeting,
chases his rubber ball into the aisle.
The front pew kneels at the communion rail,
heads bowed. Aunt Sally, reaching for the child,
bumps into Captain Randall. He goes pale
with cursing rage, jumps up, and knocks her down.
In the hush that follows, the minister proclaims,
Coloreds aren't welcome here, from this day on.
T.T.'s blue eyes meet hers, sharing her shame.
The colored worshippers, silent and grim,
file out as the organist strikes up a hymn.

VI Good Friday Prayer
Psalm 51

Defy him! Tear his organ off! Strike him
with righteous lightning! Make the devil pay!
Uncle Warren paces, has paced since Sunday,
wrestling with demons and with cherubim,
reaching for heaven, balancing on hell's rim.
Life's promise seems to him a vast array
of shit and more shit, followed by decay.
Now, on Friday evening, he kneels to pray a psalm,
remembering *His* unearned suffering,

and how He said, Forgive them. Poor, poor fools.
The spade of prayer cuts stone, untaps a spring
of clear compassion. Uncle Warren feels
God present again. *Help ME do no wrong.*
The others? Well, it's like preaching to mules.

VII Easter Sermon, 1866
Acts 10:40–43

Others might think it's like preaching to mules
to preach to dark-faced people who sign X
laboriously. They listen on cotton bales
as Uncle Warren reads from the book of Acts.
A rose-gold dawnlight streams in through the chinks
and roosters halleloo the sun's return.
In a makeshift church reeking with familiar stinks,
field hands, bricklayers, and domestics yearn
toward Jesus.
    Well, sir, like the gospels say,
only a handful saw the risen Lord:
What was true in them days still holds true today.
Be a witness. Pull the plow and sow His word.
Come harvest you'll have love you can give away,
and a heart that wells up of its own accord.

III

HERMITAGE

THE LIFE OF A SAINT

after Giotto

I The Saint Leaves His Father's House

A boy walks out
onto the sun's bright stage.
The leaves are celebrating
the resurrection of birds,
the sky shouts hallelujah.
Nothing is more real than the dust
and the cobbled streets that shine
like water under his feet.
He is off to seek his fortune,
God, in the changing faces of the year.

A saint laughs
from the boy's throat;
his father's house becomes
a small reflection in his eyes.

II The Saint's Dream

The saint gets up
in his skinny clothes.
His cave is cold and damp
as an April morning.
Even the sparrows
have found someplace to be warm.
The saint shivers to work:
he is performing penance for his eyes,
beheading all the flowers
that offend his sight.
He awakens suddenly on his feet
with his fists full of petals
and remembers his dazzling dream
of the night before.

He had entered the musical air
of the kingdom of heaven,
bared his head to the light
from five great thrones.
One throne,
fat cushions done in gold,
stood on a pedestal.

On the mountain
are only the wind
and the saint
but he hears
from the dust
like the voice of his mother,
long years dead,
someone saying,
"This was the chair of one
who would be holier than I."

III Seducing the Saint

He was so pure
he only ate white flowers.
Nobody knew what his body
smelled like. His lips
opened and closed around prayers,
his thin skin was a bag
for blood and bones and a heart
that sang, beating,
the glory of God.

I went to him once
on a morning heavy with rain
to ask why my man

was a stranger to me
and why my womb worried
itself over and over to death,
and hardly had knelt
at his punctured feet
when the dove of the Lord
entered my belly
and opened his trembling wings.

It was a revelation.
Fire leapt like dogs
from my hair,
my mouth came alive,
I could read the secrets
in the scent of his robe,
birds tingled in my fingers,
I felt the shadows melt back
in my eyes.

Folding his hands
into his sleeves,
the saint arose.
"The way of woman
leads to darkness,"
he said, and threw himself
into that thicket there.
But the roses knew me
and drew in their thorns.
Their leaves caressed him
in my name, buds burst
into ecstatic blossom
all around him.

IV The Saint Preaches

The saint has come back to town.
Everyone comes out.
His father's old retainers
whisper how he's changed.
He says he has a mistress now,
that his pride kisses the ground.
He seems so strange.
He carries his hunger
in a wooden bowl.

Some say they see his mistress,
that she's old
and wears rags. He says
he's been praying for years.
When he limps
through the streets
he leaves red footprints
for the rain to eat.
He looks as wild as the baptist,
everyone says, but they hang around
anyway when he starts to preach.

He's talking to something beyond them,
it seems, no, something so close
they'd forgotten to notice,
like their own good stink
or the beauty of kitchens.
When he opens his arms they think
birds fly out like coins.
He speaks a language they understand
but can't speak.
It sounds to them like singing,

like the melody of the wind
in the gray olive trees.

They hang around all day
and when they go home
it seems better,
as if they'd discovered salt.
They forget the dark
they're afraid of
and remember all night long
how the saint opened his wings
among the gathering birds,
how he opened his beak,
how he sang.

(For the Body)

PSALM

So many cars have driven past me
without a head-on collision.
I started counting them today:
there were a hundred and nine
on the way to the grocery,
a hundred and two on the way back home.
I got my license
when I was seventeen.
I've driven across country
at least twelve times;
I even drive
late Saturday nights.
I shall not want.

(Magnificat)

DUSTING

Thank you for these tiny
particles of ocean salt,
pearl-necklace viruses,
winged protozoans:
for the infinite,
intricate shapes
of submicroscopic
living things.

For algae spores
and fungus spores,
bonded by vital
mutual genetic cooperation,
spreading their
inseparable lives
from equator to pole.

My hand, my arm,
make sweeping circles.
Dust climbs the ladder of light.
For this infernal, endless chore,
for these eternal seeds of rain:
Thank you. For dust.

(Magnificat)

I DREAM THE BOOK OF JONAH

for Mel Nelson and Pamela Espeland

I fell asleep on the couch

One stormy April afternoon
While Roger and Jacob were shopping
I lay down on the couch and had a dream.

Lord, Lord, sang Jonah
Trouble on my mind
Lord, sweet Mama,
Trouble on my mind.
If you love me like you tell me,
Why don't you give a sign?

Jonah began his story

Well, God wakes me up from a nap on the couch
and a dream of talking to an angel,
and says
GET READY TO LEAVE IN TEN MINUTES FOR NINEVEH.
I'd heard of it once
when I was a kid,
and what I remembered wasn't pretty:
fast women on drugs,
kids rapin old ladies,
lonesome men sittin all day at the movies
with their pants unzipped.
Not this boy, I says,
and I heads out in the opposite direction,
out towards Tarshish, a city I visited one time
back durin the war.

A lot of funny things happen on the way to the port.
First an oak tree blows down
most on top of me.

Lucky for me I jumped back real quick,
but a bolt of lightnin just missed,
and the sky was a shotgun
spittin out hail
when I got to the ship.

It was stormin like crazy,
and the weather got worse.
I was soppin. The deck
was all slippery with puke.
I prayed on my knees
to a sky white with thunder,
and the other men hears me
and blames it all on me.
They says, Man look what happens
when you try to slip away from God.

Then they grabs my cash
and throws me overboard.

Then Jonah took out his guitar

Well, I was tryin to swim,
which was hard to begin with,
when the biggest old fish in the world
looms up like a freight train out of the fog.
I thought I was done for.

It was no picnic in that fish's belly.
It was hot in the first place,
and it stunk to high heaven.
There was nothin to eat,
nothin to hold on to,

nothin to breathe
but what felt like squids.
I was in there for days,
but it felt like a lifetime.
I kept my mouth up out of the slime
and I prayed like a preacher.

I woke up on a beach somewhere,
thirsty as hell.
I was glad to be alive,
I'll admit,
but I was hoppin mad.

Now Jonah began to tune his guitar

Well, the next thing I know,
here comes God gain,
saying, I TOLD YOU NINEVEH.
AND LET THIS BE A WARNING TO YOU.
Well, this time I went.

I spent a day or two walkin around,
sort of gettin the feel of the place.
It was like walkin in shit.
(Excuse me, ladies.)
I figure God's right:
this place should be cleaned up.

After a while I stops walkin.
I puts my hat on the sidewalk,
and I starts in to sing.
A crowd forms around me:
a bunch of shriveled up women
out lookin through they glasses
at the window displays.

When I sing out God's warnin to Nineveh,
they like to jump out they skins.
They leave quick and come back
with they fancy-dressed sons,
they skinny-legged daughters,
and they gun-totin men.

I can see they eyes
narrow to hate me,
and then, as I pick up the beat,
their eyes widen with fear.
Pretty soon the street in front of me,
the main street, and all of the other
busy streets in town
was full of people on they knees,
swayin and cryin and prayin
to the melody of my song.

For the next thirty days
everbody in Nineveh but me,
right on down to the lap dogs,
went without eatin.

I ate porkchops and lobsters every night.
In empty restaurants.
Alone.

And Jonah began to stroke a tentative rhythm

After a month or so,
I goes up to a hilltop
and waits.

I waits about a week.

If it hadn't been for some country folks
on the way into Nineveh for a good time,
I could of starved.

After a while I gets fed up with waitin.
I asks God why She was holdin things up,
and God says, GRACE.
Meaning mercy, I think.

I says, What?
You mean I did all that singin for nothin?
Them people is gone to be laughin off they heads!

All this trouble,
I says,
and you changed your mind?

I just wanted to die.

Now his fingers found the melody

Well, I goes out in the desert
and I sits in the sun.

Hot enough to fry lizards!

Then somethin shoots out the sand
right beside me, like a geyser,
tall as a tree.

It was a tree.
I was catchin my breath
and feelin the place in my neck
where the pulse is
when God's voice says,

RELAX. ENJOY.
So I sit in the shade.

That night I dream
about tellin my friends
how God made me a miracle
in Nineveh.
I wake up with a splittin headache,
layin right out in the sun.
The tree's just a handful of ashes.

I jumps to my feet.
Hey, that was a wonderful tree!
I yells, talkin to heaven
and kickin the sand.
Who do you think you are?

Then a voice booms so close to me
it could a been inside my head.
WHO DO YOU THINK I AM? it says.
I MADE THE TREE, AND NINEVEH,
AND YOU.
WHO THE HELL YOU THINK
YOU TALKIN TO?

So Jonah sang the blues

Lord, Lord, sweet Mama,
Trouble on my mind.
Lord, sweet Mama,
Trouble on my mind.
If you love me like you tell me,
Please, Mama, give me a sign.

You know you hard on me,
Sometimes you act like you ain't there.

Even my daddy say you hard on me,
Say you act like you ain't there.
First you say you love me,
Then you don't act like you care.

I was dreamin an angel
When you called my name.
I had a dream about an angel
When you called my name.
Now I can't go back to sleep, Mama,
Nothin is the same.

I been layin here thinkin,
Now it's almost dawn.
I been layin here thinkin,
Now it's almost dawn.
If you won't turn my knees to jelly, Mama,
Let that sweet-talkin angel
I was dreamin about
Go on.

I woke up and wrote about it

Mel, I dreamed this,
and I woke up astounded.
The living room was flooded
with the afternoon's milky light.
I rose out of that sleep
like a woman drowned.
I walked around for weeks,
going to classes, cooking,
leading my ordinary life,
but I taught my friend Pamela
like a Kiowa dreamer
the song I had learned.

And all this time the universe
was inventing its perfect colors,
the changing sky was humming
its bleak and holy music.
All this time insects
were waking up
to their brief, meaningful lives,
snakes were writhing together
in the noisy leaves under the hedge.
All this time I was being born and dying
in every cell of my body,
the birds were singing,
the April grass
for the rest of the planet's life
was curled like billions of foetuses
on the delicate stairway
of this April's DNA.

And I am a part of this graceful rhythm
with you, my brother,
the only grown man now
who shares my genes.
This dream was a journey
into the lightest continent of my heart.
And like Jonah,
like the hermit who comes out of his cave,
like the mystic,
like the woman who prays,
I've come back empty-handed,
singing,
dazed.

(Mama's Promises)

LETTER TO A BENEDICTINE MONK

Dear Frère Jacques,
Every night a new loneliness:
So much love for the lost.
And once or twice a month for more than twenty years
I've dreamed of a lost boy
and waked an unnameable ache.

When we met at a party
morning bells rang
at first sight.
He kissed my hand,
looked into my eyes,
said he'd never cease
loving me.
His white shirt and pants,
the sunkissed wave
curving over his brow:
I answered his open gaze
with an equal promise.

I prowled past his house many midnights
like a cat in season.
We seemed to be friends:
We both wrote poems;
we waved on campus;
sometimes we talked:
whenever we met
that same silver tingle
rang in my chest.

Once, he asked me out.
We drove in circles for hours, lost
on the way to a drive-in,
confused by the road map,
the roads, and the warmth

a few inches away.
We drove home in silence.
"Don't say anything," he said;
"Don't get up."
He left me posed,
a black madonna,
on my livingroom floor.
I'd waited two years
for the kiss he withheld.

One summer evening
just after we graduated,
some of my friends came over
for wine and cheese.
We were moving, taking off
for what we called Real Life.
This was his last American night.
He was staying with someone
whose name I didn't catch.
Nonchalant as you please
on the floor in front of the couch,
knowing I'd die
if I didn't touch him,
my heart stopped as stone in my mouth,
as everyone got up to go
I placed one hand
on his foot.

The last guest to leave,
he turned in my doorway:
"Will you sleep with me?"

My laughter.
I've been waiting for you

all this time,
and now it's impossible,
it's too late,
at last,
yes:
it meant. And the boy ran
to his motorbike and roared
into the road before I stopped
laughing.

I ran after, crying his name,
but *ex machina* a freight train
muted my voice.
He didn't look back.

Frère Jacques,
I think of you often,
and pray you are happy and well.
What a search it has been.
Forgive me. I loved him.
But perhaps you don't
remember me at all.

(Magnificat)

THE PRAYER OF SILENCE

I've fought off the octopi and the Great White Shark,
and drifted into silence:
On the far wall a glass-brick cross
filters early morning light.
A veteran candle on the low altar,
a jar of dried grasses,
a painted cross on an easel,
a sad-eyed ikon
of a woman
holding a baby.
High on the right wall
a plain wooden cross.
A man on a wicker stool,
his head bowed,
his hands folded.

He stands, open his arms,
looks up, closes his eyes,
and takes in
radiance.

(Magnificat)

THE FRUIT OF FAITH

Abba Jacob, on the word
of his master,
planted a walking-stick
and watered it every day
for seven years.
In the seventh year it grew leaves.
In the eighth it produced
a wholly new fruit.

Come,
says the master.
Partake.

(Magnificat)

ABBA JACOB AND MIRACLES

One day Abba Jacob
was praying in a sunbeam
by the door to his underground cell,
and the brethren came to him
to ask him about miracles.
One of the elders said,
My mother's spirit came back
and turned out all the lights
the night we gathered for her wake:
Was that a miracle?
Another said, One spring evening
a white rainbow of mist
passed over our heads:
Was that a miracle?
They went on like this
for several hours.
Abba Jacob listened.
Then there was silence.

Big deal,
said Abba Jacob.
Miracles happen all the time.
We're here,
aren't we?

(Magnificat)

FISH AND FLOOR-DUST BOUQUET

Abba Jacob hums quietly, negotiating traffic
from the airport, white sleeves rolled back
from his tanned hands on the wheel, white skirt
from belt to barefoot sandals on the pedals.
Amma Mama hums, too, watching landscapes grow and go.
A truck has stopped on the edge of the highway,
its load of fish spilled, its driver laughing,
fish on the pavement and grass as laughing men
toss silver arcs back into the truck or ride off
on mopeds and bicycles with fish on their laps,
in baskets, fish under their arms. For a passing
moment, the air seems to flash with fish, and happy yells
join two old fools' humming. They exchange a quick,
delighted glance. They are driving to his place:
a fieldstone monastery surrounded by wind-rattled cane.
The guesthouse has a new veranda, the well
is twenty meters deep, there's a pool with little carp,
and three sheep now mow weeds near the hidden hermitage.
When Amma Mama has seen everything, Abba Jacob walks her
to her room and bows outside her door. He says: I'd planned
to have flowers here for you, and everything
clean and fresh. But I was called away
before I finished sweeping, so you have
a pile of dust in the middle of the floor.
That's much more symbolic, don't you think?
Mass is at five.

Amma Mama bows, laughing, and straightens
to watch him walk away. She remembers
his shoulders. Fish everywhere,
fish like sunlight from the afternoon sky.

ABBA JACOB AND THE BUSINESSMAN

A businessman heard about Abba Jacob
and went to see him
about his difficulties
with mental prayer.
Abba Jacob
was planting trees.
When the businessman saw him
he said, Boy,
tell me where the cell
of Abba Jacob is.
Abba Jacob said:
What do you want with him?
The man is a fool.

Oh, said the businessman,
turning away.
I heard he
was holy.

(Magnificat)

ABBA JACOB AND THE THEOLOGIAN

Thanking him for spending
the entire afternoon
and half the dinner hour
discussing the various ramifications
of the essentially paradoxical nature
of faith,
the theologian interrupts her first
spoonful of lentils
to lean forward again
and cut off
the flow of God.
Reverend Father, she asks,
what is the highest spiritual virtue?

Abba Jacob looks to heaven
and groans.
Humor, he says.
Not seriously, of course.

(Magnificat)

ABBA JACOB AND ST. FRANCIS

Abba Jacob with his invention—
a flashlight lantern on a cord around his neck—
balances tiptoe on an upended barrel.
There's one,
he mutters, and reaches.
The damned creatures
are making lace
of my arbor.
He holds each beetle for a moment,
then breaks it and tosses it aside.
The watching guests,
laughing, tease him:
So much for St. Francis.

Abba Jacob says:
Well, at least I don't call them
brother
and *then* kill them.

But I do
ask God's pardon.

(Magnificat)

ABBA JACOB AND THE ANGEL

homage to Henri Cartier-Bresson

In the end Abba Jacob gave up
trying to wrestle with the angel.
She was stronger than he,
and a full head
wiser.
He panted
against her shoulder
as she took his hand in hers
and put her arm around his neck.
Then he heard the music.

(Magnificat)

BLESSING THE BOATS

Abba Jacob said:
Did I ever tell you about the time
I was asked to bless the fishing boats?
I got to the appointed beach at the appointed time,
in my long white tunic, of course, and discovered
the beach had been taken over by a crowd
of Italian tourists, most of them women, and topless.
Luckily—or unluckily for me,
considering the circumstances—they were all
beautiful. One or two of them . . .
Well, what could I do?
I just walked through them.
They parted before me
like the waves of the Red Sea, silent
and watching. It was almost all I could do
to keep a straight face
and look straight ahead.
I thought such a fancy-dressed audience
deserved a grand gesture,
so I walked right in, shoes and all,
to my chest in the sea.
Inwardly bursting with laughter,
I stroked the nearest prow
and blessed the boats
with the sign of the Cross.
Then I turned and blessed the beach.

I didn't laugh until I got home.
They're probably still
talking about it.

ABBA JACOB'S ASIDE ON HELL

Abba Jacob said:
I wonder if souls are unhappy
in hell.
I rather doubt it.
And if they are
they won't admit it,
like people in an expensive nightclub,
glad-handed by the rich and beautiful,
while the rich
and the beautiful
hold cold hands
to a fire in a dustbin.

(Magnificat)

MEN IN THE KITCHEN

I

Abba Jacob said:
I scooped some dying fish
from the carp pond this evening;
they were a little bit smelly,
but I think they're okay.
I'm going to cook them for the dogs.

II

Abba Jacob said: Well, I've buried them
and aired the place out.
I've heard candles remove odors. I'll light these.
I think I'll make an omelette for our supper.

(Amma Mama said, How romantic:
Cooking by candlelight!)

III

Abba Jacob said: Seat in zee chair,
ent I shall demonstrate
how vee prepare zee perfect omelette.
First vee varm zee pan.
Zen vee att a beat of zee butter.
Zen vee break zee ecks . . .
Oh, my goodness! What a stench!

IV

Abba Jacob said: Well, I've buried them.
At least the windows
were already open.

(Amma Mama said, I hope you realize
this gives women several thousand points.)

Abba Jacob said: I let you have them:
You've been falling terribly behind.

V

Abba Jacob said: Thank You
for the delicious meal we are about to share,
and for meals we have shared and will share,
and for meals shared with others we love.
Thank You for the perfect meal we shall someday
share in full communion, dissolved in You
as laughter dissolves in laughter.

VI

Abba Jacob said:
Have I ever told you
about my ancestor the corsair?
He was so wicked he once kidnapped
his own mother and held her for ransom.

ABBA JACOB'S SEVEN DEVILS

Another miracle
comes knocking at his door,
crying Father.
Another penitent,
another seeker,
another love.
He puts her up
in the guesthouse
and calls it
The Queen's Palace.
The last sleeper in its bed
a worn hooker
he found in the street.
She says he's a saint,
too.
        All night the dogs howl.

(Magnificat)

CLOWN NOSE

After their afternoon walk to the sheepfold
Amma Mama waited on the stone wall.
Abba Jacob reappeared on the guesthouse veranda
wearing his mended tunic, a tennis visor, a clown nose.
He led the dogs in laughing zigzags on the grass, then sat
at her feet, twirling the clown nose in his fingers.

Abba Jacob said:
In the monastery, they still used the discipline:
You could sign out a hair shirt or a little whip.
I tried it once or twice; it never did anything
for me. But a couple of the novices whipped themselves
every night. (They'd obviously
never read Freud.)
One of the brothers had an old leather suitcase
he used to cover with a blanket
and whip past midnight, moaning.

Several men have wanted to join me here,
but I turned them all away.
I don't think they were cut out for it.
The solitary life can be difficult.
Each of them insisted he felt called,
and I'm sure they were.
But the call isn't to a specific life:
It's to the Absolute.
Everyone gets that call.
Answering it doesn't mean
you have to renounce the world
and live on one bean a day.
All you have to do
is seek to see clearly, to see reality.
And the ultimate reality, of course,
is God.

Abba Jacob fell silent.
He put on the clown nose, hopped up,
brushed off his white skirt.

ABBA JACOB AT BAT

A young visitor
wearing an Angels cap
sat down cross-legged
at Abba Jacob's feet.
Abba Jacob said:
That baseball cap
reminds me of the man who died in my arms
when I was twenty-three.
His last words were
Put out the light.

Why baseball caps?
Abba Jacob rose and took his guest's cap,
snapped it twice against his forearm,
put it on, and straightened the peak.
He said: Because they remind us
to live.

(Magnificat)

I KNEW THAT

for Judy Maines-La Marre

In his miraculously fixed
crap game Job came out
with a better life,
said Abba Jacob.
(Yes, and what about his wife,
Amma Mama said;
could new children
replace the old?)

Abba Jacob said:
The God of the Book of Job
is the God of Job's
uncomprehending friends.
God's not like that.
God's not a manipulator.
I wouldn't serve
a God like that: I'd rather serve
the devil. (Though the devil might
be even worse, a real rationalizer.)

The answer God really gives Job
is Christ. Christ is God's way
of telling us that,
in becoming one of us,
in sharing our pain,
God suffers; God dies.

(Amma Mama pointed out
that there are whole races of Jobs:
Africans, Tribal Americans,
Australian Aborigines . . .
How can God choose one race,
while allowing the slavery
of other races to lead to nothing

but further slavery, she asked.
The slavery of the Jews,
she noted, was redeemed, after all:
but what about ours? Surely peoples
of color all over the world
have a right to rail
against God's perverted sense of justice.
What answer does God give them?)

Abba Jacob looked at her
and raised his eyebrows.
(Oh, said Amma Mama.)

AT PRAYER

Abba Jacob closes the prayer book,
sets his glasses aside.
He smiles at Amma Mama, turns,
and gazes into the air
a few centimenters above the altar.

In the oratory's sea-bottom silence
she can almost hear her blood's
circling; wind in the palms surrenders
to the whirr the ears hear under sound.
With each breath a gate swings: open, shut.

You could, if you closed your eyes,
almost slide into that tilted gaze,
into the radiance
of Abba Jacob's prayer.
You could almost be here.

The door bangs open, pushed by a nose,
and Abba Jacob's three little dogs trot in,
stand a moment in his gentle regard,
scratch, yawn, and curl into sleep
around his white skirts.

THE SIMPLE WISDOM

Abba Jacob said:
There's a big difference between
the mentalities of magic and of alliance.
People who spend their lives searching for God
have a magical mentality: They need a sign, a proof,
a puff of smoke, an irrefutable miracle.
People who have an alliance mentality
know God by loving.

ABBA JACOB GETS DOWN

Abba Jacob said:
There was once a Desert Father
who had a bad novice.
One day the novice died
and went to hell.
That night the abba
went into ecstasy:
He had a vision of his novice
surrounded by fire.
My son, he said, I pity you
for being there.

That's all right, Father,
the novice replied.
I'm sitting
on three bishops.

(Magnificat)

DON'T THROW OUT WINE BOTTLES

Abba Jacob said: When I was in grad school, I house-sat
a beautiful modern house on stilts beside a river
for a brilliant professor known to be a virago. She left
a detailed typewritten list, three pages long,
of things I was to do: water plants, play with the cat . . .
The last thing on the list, in caps and underlined,
was DON'T THROW OUT WINE BOTTLES.
I wondered why, shrugged, and lived for four months
following her instructions to the letter.
I drank a lot of wine in those days
and by the end of four months had more than a hundred
empty bottles stashed here and there around the house;
first in kitchen cabinets, then in the closets, then
in the laundry hamper, a desk drawer, under the bed,
wherever I found space. I spent two days cleaning,
and when she came back the house was perfect.
I moved happily back into my college.

She telephoned later that same day, furious:
What the hell did I think I was doing,
leaving her with all those goddamn wine bottles?
She demanded I come and get them.
Immediately. Or she'd sue.
I begged a friend to go with me;
he knew her by reputation and was terrified,
but he was a good friend, and he had a car.
On the river road to her house he said
maybe she wouldn't kill us if we were together.
I'd bought flowers, and when we got there
I handed them to her without a word.
With her arms clenched across her chest,
one hand dangling the bouquet, she glared
as we clumped upstairs and down
with bags and boxes of bottles.
She must have thought I was mad.

I never dared to ask
what DON'T THROW OUT WINE BOTTLES meant.
Maybe it had some deep,
esoteric meaning.

LAUGHTER AS THE HIGHEST FORM OF CONTEMPLATION

Abba Jacob said:
Do you know anything about Zen?
Can a *koan* be a question? Can it be funny?
I've been thinking I ought to give you
something to contemplate
that would make you laugh.

(Amma Mama ventured, Well,
there's the famous *koan*: "What is the sound
of one hand clapping?" That's a question.)

Has anyone answered that question?
Abba Jacob asked, and laughed:
There's your *koan*.

LEAVING THE HOSPICE

for Robert and Patrice Pfeffer

Abba Jacob said:
It's amazing: The old nun has been resurrected!
It was so clear last night that she was ready
to die. I hope her doctors haven't made her labor
more difficult. We all have to die, you know,
when we've reached the end of our lives. The lucky
prepare themselves, clean house, so to speak, make peace.
Our clinging to the old like selfish children afraid
to be left alone in the dark must make leave-taking arduous.
Does our medicine prolong their living, or their dying?
What awaits is welcome purer than true love's first kiss.

ACHES AND PAINS

Abba Jacob said:
The older I get, the more clearly I believe
that old age is the desert.
It's biblical, too. In youth
we are the Jews in Egypt,
convinced that gifts
come horizontally: from other men,
like documents of manumission,
or from the land, like river water
and golden-headed, flowing grain.
Grown older we know, a people adrift
in a featureless wasteland,
that all gifts come from heaven.
Like manna. Like respite. Like rain.

POST-PRANDIAL CONVERSATION

Abba Jacob said:
I'm sorry; I forgot. I'm always forgetting things.
The Wednesday morning mass, for instance.
It's an early mass, right after my morning prayer,
and sometimes I forget myself so deeply I'm late,
or I don't make it to mass at all.
It's happened so often the parish council
has suggested the police
might fetch me every Wednesday,
with flashing lights and sirens.
I've always been a bit absentminded.
When I was in England once I invited a friend's mother,
an old lady as absentminded as I, to lunch in my flat.
On the date of our engagement I forgot, and went out.
She remembered the date and the time and the numbers
of my address, but went to the house on the next street over.
She knocked; there was no answer. She assumed I'd ducked out
and would return soon with something I'd forgotten:
chutney, perhaps. She tried the door, found it unlocked,
and went in to wait. Meanwhile, gazing from a bus window,
I suddenly remembered. I jumped off the bus, ran
to the nearest florist, and bought every flower they had:
a bouquet so large I could barely see around it.
I sat blushing on the bus to Mrs. Piggott's street
while everyone smiled at me. I stumbled off and felt
my way toward her flat. She had sat in the wrong house
for almost an hour, and had finally decided
she must have come on the wrong day.
She arrived at her home a few seconds
before I, blinded by flowers,
raced into her courtyard, slipped,
and fell flat on my face in a mud-puddle.
The flowers were ruined.

I've told the Wednesday people that
if I don't come, they should spend the hour
forgetting themselves . . .

Abba Jacob sat long minutes, staring into space.
At last he rose, said *Amen, Alleluia,*
bowed to Amma Mama, and strode away.
The screen door of the oratory creaked.
Then there was only the om of mosquitos.

MAY YOUR LOVE CONVERT LUCIFER

Even the devil has some good in him.
                              —*St. Anthony*

Abba Jacob said: I pray for Lucifer.
I rather like him, you know. My moral
theology professor once said God hates Satan.
I said I hope that's not true:
If God hates Satan, God must hate me, too,
because I am a sinner. But God loves me.
If the devil has anything to do with half
the hate and evil that goes on in the world,
as it seems he does, then he is a terrifying being.
On the other hand, his power was broken
by Christ's great gifts of love and life,
and he was created good and beautiful,
and God still loves him.
Why, then, should we hate him?

So I pray for him once in a while,
when I think of it.
I'll bet it makes him
mad as hell.

LOVESONG

after Rilke

How shall I hold my spirit, that it not
touch yours? How shall I send it soaring past
your height into the patient waiting, there
above you? Oh, if only I could shut
it up, leave it to gather velvet dust
someplace where it would echo you no more.
But, like two strings vibrating as the bow
ripples them with a long, caressing stroke,
we tremble, drawn together by one joy.
What instrument is this? Whose fingers make
a chord beyond our capacity for awe?
How sweet, how: *Ah!*

(Magnificat)

ABBA JACOB IN THE WELL

Bakar, Atul, and Clancy lower a bucket
and raise it slowed by stones.
Once in a while Clancy turns on the pump
to see whether water is running now, or mud.
As they pay the rope downward they call
questions, suggestions to a dark cloud
moving slowly among sky reflections.
They harken to the intelligible melody
of sifted water and Abba Jacob's voice,
as he returns the bucket filled with muddy pebbles.
Oui, mon père. The four work quietly together,
who dug the well with pick and shovel,
who are building a stone tower beside it
where Abba Jacob will bring his prayer.
Tomorrow they'll work again on the chapel.
The ladder cuts through slanting light
and disappears.

A CANTICLE FOR ABBA JACOB

1

How beautiful you are, my love,
how beautiful you are. I always knew
you were a redwood in a grove
of mangos; shadows under you
fragranced, cool as an Easter morning's dew.

2

Twelve thousand miles. He sees me first,
and calls me. And his eyes are just the same.
I don't know which of these is worse:
the joy of turning toward my name,
or the pain of smothering a rising flame.

3

He talks about a helpless God;
walking with me, he holds up his white hem.
He listens, smiles, and nods. The God
of the Desert Father's apothegms,
who seeks the poor, who lights the world through them.

4

At lunch in the refectory
he feeds me from a papaya with his spoon.
Joy curves in a trajectory
which I visualize as a cartoon
of a contrail fading miles beyond the moon.

5

A paring knife slices my thumb.
He jumps up, takes the bandage from my hand,
and binds it. I feel, yielding, dumb,
his tenderness and his command.
His dark hair . . . We step back. We understand.

6

The territory-marking calls
of morning birds divide darkness from day.
Within white oratory walls
a hermit and a mother pray.
They pray in silence. God knows what they say.

7

Ad te clamamus exsules . . .
How perfectly plainsong's twin poles combine
to raise the soul's lamenting praise,
its joyous heartbreak.
                          I incline
my head and chant: Beloved, I am thine.

8

My Love is coming toward my room.
Like Cinderella on her wedding night,
who waits, breathing her own perfume,
I tremble, heartsick with delight.
The Bridegroom comes. His gentle eyes. His might.

9

I sleep, but my night-watching heart
hears my Beloved calling through the door.
I run to force steel bars apart
and open to Him. But before
I breathe free air He's not there anymore.

10

I seek Him on my bed whom my
heart loves. Impossible. I cannot find
a trace under the curving sky.
And still I cannot stop my mind
searching for Him who left my heart behind.

11

How beautiful You are, my Love,
how beautiful You are.

Your changeful eyes,
the humble grace with which you move
your hands, your laughter, your surprise.
Your listening silences. Your God, who dies.

12

He nestles me in His embrace.
Don't rouse my Love. My breath mingles with His.

The quiet contours of his face:
Touch them as I would. I pray this.
Touch him for me, my Lord.

My Love! Thy kiss!

(Magnificat)

THE PLOTINUS SUITE

I No Jazz

Hard sex. The silken, honeyed twang of parting.
No effing jazz. A violin, a tad too white.
Rough sex. More sex.
                    Okay, then: Radio silence.
Silence, longing. Never his scent
in my nostrils, his tongue
tasting mine, his smooth . . . Ah, it comes:

Those to whom heaven-passion
is unknown may only guess at it
by the passions of the earth.

Abba Jacob watched a porn film for a few minutes once,
in a monastery on midnight TV. It was sad, he said;
they looked so lonely.

II Behind a Descartes Bumpersticker

. . . therefore I am? That's not it either.
I love? Could be. A slightly pregnant pause.
How love? And whom? Your faces file in,

quietly take seats, listen. My hoping eyes
scour the horizon. Where is he
whom my essence it is to love?

Our true beloved is elsewhere.
Abba Jacob says there's a little door in the heart
behind which he is hidden.

Even if it bears someone's name,
on a whiff through the keyhole
catch the faint spring fragrance of longing . . .

III To San Francisco

Trunks clunk together behind me and Dora,
full of books, letters, seashells, pottery, stones,
memories, lies I tell myself: A future tag-sale.

Jake and Roger walk, talking scores.
Spare us that debate in the desert
of what stays, what goes. Spare me

the haunted clarity of the survivor
wading down from the thawing pass.
I am dust. I leave a trail of offerings.

Take this, this. My glittering illusions,
my ambition, my pride, but not . . .

Take away everything.

IV The Jesus Prayer

You ought not to ask,
but to understand
in silence.

Have mercy compels each cricket,
each pell-mell thought, the cosmos known
and imagined, to circle in yearning.

If I could go all the way,
beyond sobbing hunger, what might I hear?
Why can't I shut up

that treeful of grackles,
the newsreels and coming attractions,
the camcorder clicking in memories, and just be still?

V Prayer of Singing Joy

Tides of the mantra shore against your silence,
but a little flick of the cortex, and I'm just
pretending to pray.

I pinch off the pink buds
of explicitly sexual fantasy,
take twenty deep breaths,

and when I've finished singing in the east-lit fields,
walk back toward the tiny oratory.
He's still standing there,

his arms outspread.
Caught up, poised in the void,
he has attained to quiet.

VI Hermitage Breakfast

For that hour he is enkindled.
I tiptoe past, put on water for tea,
set the table for two.

He comes in radiant
as a morning-after bridegroom.
Some things one need not ask.

He blesses the table; we sit
to yesterday's tough bread,
steam rising from two cups.

Once in a while he looks at me and smiles.
I know: It was winged light;
it was love's incandescent center.

VII Sneak Preview

The door burst open into a cathedral
filled with   loving light.
Beyond arched windows

in far deep   interior space,
for one fibrillation of a wave of electromagnetic radiation
I was there, extinguished.

I awakened out of the body to myself.
Then I was at my desk,
murmuring, "Oh. I see."

It's just like everyone
says. There's a big
                      light

VIII The True Magic

I had all but one of the family pictures
needed to divide the sections in my last book,
but I couldn't find one of my dad as a Tuskegee cadet.

Two days before the publisher's deadline, my cousin called
to say something weird had happened to him the night before.
He'd gone to his first meeting of Tuskegee Airmen, Inc.

The stranger sitting beside him had asked his connection
to the original group, and Roy had told him Daddy's name.
Oh, said the man; then I guess this must be for you.

Daddy's eyes are looking straight into the camera.
The true magic is the love contained within the universe.
This is the original enchanter.

IX Parable of the Moth

A heliotropic moth looked up
from the screen one June moon evening
and fell into impossible longing.

He couldn't eat, couldn't sleep.
Blear-eyed on the third noon
he looked up again, into the sun.

His first experience was loving
a great luminary
by means of some thin gleam from it.

Hallowed be, he proclaimed,
and fell into a stupor.
That night he was back at the screen.

X *Enneads,* I, vi

How do we get to that promised motherland?
What star should we follow?
You can't get there on foot;

your feet only carry you everywhere
in this world, from country to country.
You can't get there by land, sea, or air.

Shut up, close your eyes,
and wake to a new way of seeing.
Go into yourself, look around.

And if what you see there isn't beautiful,
don't stop smoothing, polishing, cutting away until
you are *wholly yourself, nothing but pure light.*

XI Union Apprehended

As facing mirrors clarify each other,
reflecting only light, the shared glance
of those made poor by love reflects union.

What is union?
This pen-light I aim into the afternoon:
Where is its beam? It is in union.

Or again: thunder. Lightning casts white nets.
At what point does the sky become the pond?
They are not two. They are union.

Your breath, the universe:
Where does one end and the other begin?
Close your eyes. *Ascend into yourself.*

XII Icarus Dream

Our Jake at three woke up one morning
asking to be dressed so he could go out
and fly. Wide-armed, he ran in circles

for a minute or two; when he came back in,
he no longer believed. Some of us given wings
fly straight to the center of radiant welcome.

An inner, inexorable magnetic north shows the way,
through rings of silence, from solitude
to solitude. The horizon of infinite mystery

is reached in stillness, through an open heart.
If love is a key, I give you mine for Abba Jacob.
Here: Make *the flight of the alone to the Alone.*

(Magnificat)

162

THE WAR OF THE HEART

Abba Pambo said, "After a monk has fought
all of the other wars, there still remains
the war of the heart."

The Snows of Kilimanjaro we planted
near the refectory door is blooming.
And last night's shouting match,
which made me close my eyes and count to ten,
broke this morning in a shared smile over the hubbub.
I knock wood for our good health,
our leak-proofed roof, our surfeit of plenty.
Our shoulders almost touched as we walked,
his hands at his back and mine in my skirt pockets,
both of us laughing.

I bounce from love to love in a cloud of wonder:
Jake's deepening giggle, the curve of Dora's eyebrows.
Impossible Roger, more my husband every day. I say,
I'll be with you in a minute, then peek
into memory like a thief with a pouch of hidden jewels.
I close my eyes and call across brown veld distance,
with an alligator puppet on my hand whom Dora is telling
the story of the ugly duckling. Knowing
I must not long for him. I must not write.
He said, The joy we feel is just a little taste!

Meanwhile he speaks in answering silence.
He sits for a long time without moving during vespers,
then looks up at the ikon and sings the Salve Regina.
He said, In the greatest love, the lovers reach
together toward God. He said, Love is simple.
He said he always seemed to step in dogshit
just before he got to my door; he used to come in,
and toss his shoes out the window before he said hello.
He said, I'll sing a Gloria, because in making you, God
seems for once to have done something pretty well.

So is love a harmonic conjunction of ionized hormones,
or a gesture which creates that toward which it points?
Or a spontaneous decision to believe, made looking
at the joy-star in somebody's eyes?
I hesitated a moment when we met, then leapt
beyond doubt. And look what faith got me:
A weird, almost non-relationship
with an inscrutable, cantankerous old hermit.
Who writes, My deep friendship extends
to everyone you love.

(Magnificat)

MEMENTO

Somewhere in France a vacation album
has a snapshot of, you guessed it, Abba Jacob,
sitting on the grass after eight o'clock mass.
White cassock and green stole he leaned forward,
head bowed, to hear a child's first confession.
On her eight braids eight white ribbons;
small hands clasped in her white chiffon lap.
A nest of quiet, a pool of white stillness
her brown face, his loving listening. Behind them
sky, sea, three sailboats.

IV

STILL FAITH

AS SIMPLE AS THAT

Talk about Bosnia led to the Hutu and Tutsi, two
peoples at each other's throats since time began,
the Tutsi lording it over Hutu vassals without shedding
their blood until the Germans turned Tutsi nobles
into bootlickers who took orders and handed them down,
then the Belgians converted the Tutsi court to bureaucratic,
authoritarian tyrants, and then with independence
came Hutu rebellion and years of periodic massacres,
thousands slaughtered, rivers clogged with the dead.

Abba Jacob said:
There was a man, Miringi, who used to cook for us
on the farm when I was a boy.
When he left us he bought a tiny bark boat
and fished the river. His wife sold the fish
at the village market. About ten years later I saw him
riding a bicycle with a cardboard box tied on in back.
I stopped to say hello, and asked Miringi how he was.
"Not too well," he replied. It seemed his brother
had been in a fight, and had been beheaded
with a cane-cutting knife. Miringi was on his way
to the magistrate's office to report the murder.
His brother's head was in the box.

Abba Jacob said:
Frightening, the atrocities we commit and bear.
I know I'm capable of horrors. I feel it sometimes:
the power, not the will. But as long as I remain
in communion with Christ through prayer,
love holds me back.

APRIL RAPE

Bessie Altmann is home again,
locked in so tight she can't take a breath,
the mouths of all the locks in the house
snatch at her like cats.

But she wants it this way.
She likes the house tight as a skin
corset around her waist,
no breeze to wrap fingers there
and whisper like he did
please please please.

Bessie Altmann avoids mirrors,
dark eyes that look into hers:
Let me go.

It is April in Philadelphia,
in her two rooms she breathes
and breathes again her body's smell.
She wants to hide in a book,
small enough to slip unnoticed
between the lines of black print
and never be seen again.

She considers alternatives:
A knife. A razor blade tucked
neatly between lip and gum.
Karate. Mace. A gun.
But she knows these will never work.

She is trying to grow teeth everywhere.
She will bite the next man that comes,
eat him up like a piece of ice.
She is glad to be home again.

(For the Body)

IS SHE OKAY?

Easy to forget the little lies: I'll call you,
let's do lunch, I promise. Then all at once
you're hearing yourself say you'll stick by her,
you'll marry her, there's no need to worry, she
won't be alone, and you're up to here in hot water.
Clean-shaven, natty and trust-me handsome
in your Levi's and linen, you're really sorry;
you meant to call her back; it was just more
than you could handle at that point in your
life. You still think about her once in a while.
Only you and she know. And she remembers what it was
to stand up in a silent room when her name was called.
She remembers the hard eyes of the Jesus Saves people.
She remembers what one woman said.

BOYS IN THE PARK

Chicago, 1967

In town to do good works, filled with our own
virtue, five of us joined a game of catch
with boys who looked like the boys who'd teased
us at recess, who called girls dumb, yanked pigtails,
burped, and were generally as annoying as younger
brothers. But, barely chest-high, these were a swarm
of fingerling piranhas, of little proto
rapists in t-shirts and sneakers, racing around us
with knowing hands, then running off
down the parkslope, tossing the ball,
laughing, children of our people, leaving us
to our shame.

Yes, they had poverty, futility,
unequal opportunity, childhood
neglect and abuse; they had hopelessness,
the past and future an unrelieved sentence
of humiliation and meaningless;
they had understandable grievances
against a society which treats some
with unjust contempt. (In yesterday's news
a samaritan walked six blocks to buy
gas for three people stranded in their car.
They threw it on him and tossed a lit match.
He was black, they were white, one was pregnant.)
And we had been sheltered by white-collar
fathers who insisted on A's, mothers
who read Langston Hughes aloud at bedtime.
Innocent as midwest hicktown white girls,
we had love, homes, hope. We had all the luck.
But is virtue the flip side of blessing?
Is malevolence excused by despair?

Engulfed in a stormcloud of boys, I looked down
on twenty close-shorn heads. In an instant I remembered
Dr. King's voice from the pulpit:
Freedom, hands rose under my skirt;
equality, my breasts were pinched.
The day before, I'd knelt on a sidewalk
singing, and a woman pushing a stroller
had called me a cocksucking nigger whore.
Justice I willed myself *peace* to unknow
conscience the evil I saw *dignity*
pinpricked in her *faith* blue *humanity* eyes.
They were boys, just boys, nine or ten years old.

IMPALA

On ballerina legs the dominant male commands the vista.
His females bow to graze sparse green, all delicate curves
and white haunches. Subordinate males haunt the periphery;
only the dominant male will mate, his offspring be future.
Two men are friends, their wives sisters. X supplies Y
with drinks, pats him on the back, lends him money, laughs
at his loud jokes. In return, Y drinks X's wine, sleeps
with X's wife, then sleeps with X's ten-year-old daughter.
None of them mentions it. The dominant male pushes his chair
away from the table, tells X how lucky he is, winks, stands.
Strokes the child's thin nape. The sisters are jealous.
Is survival of the fittest evil, or just natural?
X offers Y another drink. He sips slowly, wondering
which one of them the lions will take first.

BEAUTY SHOPPE

Yes, girl, he was fine. All night he'd groan I love you
baby, marry me, let me do it to you: Girl, he made my toes
curl. Then he got transferred. I quit my job, put my
furniture in storage, took my son out of school like a fool,
and waited for him to come back and get me. After a couple
of weeks, I got worried. Come a month of his silence,
I was praying he hadn't got himself killed. I called
his barracks every night, but they always said he was out.
After nights of calling I'd got to know the voice
of this white boy who said I'm sorry to tell you this,
Alberta, but he's been here every time you've called.
He won't come to the phone. All of the other Negro
guys are laughing at you. You shouldn't call again;
he's not worth it. Girl, that nigger broke my heart.

APE-GODS

from the Danish of Thorkild Bjørnvig

1

Vivisection is up to date.
Now they not only cut open the living creature,
remove glands, liver, eyes, infect it
with fatal diseases—for the sake of medicine.
These are the procedures of yesterday and the day before.
Now they not only inject beneficial poisons
employed in homes and gardens, used
in face creams and for military purposes.
They experiment not only with cold, heat, and electric shock
to find out how much an organism can take
before death intervenes. No, now vivisection
undertakes psychological
experiments on animals.

For example, the study of
maternal deprivation
(separation from the mother)
and the effects
upon newborn baby monkeys
of total isolation—
not only from mother and other monkeys,
but, as the study emphasizes, from every living creature,
human as well as subhuman
(sub-human).
The isolation continued
from a few hours after birth
until they were 3, 6, or 12 months old,
and it produced
(Here I quote from the journal):
A wide range of abnormal behaviors—
bizarre locomotions,
increased vocalization,

stereotypic behavior patterns,
self-biting,
self-clasping of the body,
self-rubbing,
self-harm,
autoeroticism—
until each settled into
its favorite form of abnormal behavior
by the time it was seven months old.
In other words: Dread.
But the study also attempted to produce
terminal depression and psychopathy,
"psychological death," it was called.
As follows:

Take a monkey baby
which has a mother—
but what kind of mother?
One that returns nothing, gives nothing.
No milk, no tenderness.
Only stiffness, only movements
away. Only terrifying rejection.
And it has nothing else—
can't begin to understand,
is a bundle of sensations whose only
hunger, cry, thirst, need
is for a mother, nothing thinkable, felt
above, beyond, under
the mother—
But words which concern feelings can only trace
the outline of this creature,
cast into the abyss, born blind
(like us all) to the first deception.

Let me therefore refer to
Harlow and Suomi's
description of their experiments
at the Primate Research Center, Madison, Wisconsin.
They constructed fabric-covered
surrogate mothers, which the infants
clung to, but which suddenly
became monsters. As follows:

The first, at regular intervals, blasted compressed air
which practically blew the skin off the baby.
But what did it do?
It clung more and more closely to the mother
because it was now a frightened baby.
It didn't become psychopathic.
But, as they maintained, "We didn't give up."
The second surrogate mother they constructed
shook the baby so violently its head
whirled around and its teeth clattered.
But the baby only held more tightly
to the mother disguise.

The third mother monster shot a wire frame
out of its belly, so the baby was thrown to the floor.
The fourth mother monster raised sharp
brass spines over its entire body, like the back
of a porcupine ("our porcupine mother," they called
the result of their teamwork, with a certain
fond pride). But see if the baby,
whatever happened, didn't climb up again, undaunted,
as soon as the wire frame and the spines
were retracted.
Better a monster mother
than no mother.
So the experiment failed.
But, as they announced in the journal,

this was not so surprising, since an injured child's
refuge must be, of course, the mother.

Finally Harlow and Suomi found the way: namely
the preparation of a living monkey mother
who was a monster. Female monkeys were raised
in absolute isolation, impregnated
while bound to a wire rack: "the rape-rack,"
so they wouldn't know the males.
They either ignored their newborns, which cried for
the teat and care. Or they crunched the baby's skull
("a favorite trick," it was called) between their teeth.
But the really sick behavior pattern, it was noted,
was to smash the baby's head against the floor
and scrub it back and forth.
Nothing appears in the report of whether the babies, if they
survived at all, tried again.

2

Because one has, for a situation of extreme
helplessness and hopelessness in people, for depression,
an image: to be sunk down in
a well of despair
(or a shaft, the depths of despair),
Harlow and Suomi tried,
moved by this image,
"on an intuitive basis," they scientifically note,
to design and create
such a well. They constructed
a shaftlike room with stainless steel
walls sloping down to
a concave floor. Young monkeys were placed
in it for periods of up to a month and a half.

After a couple of days' stay there, they
spent most of their time hunched up

against a wall in the shaft room—
and even nine months after they were removed
the same monkeys sat motionless,
their arms clenched in self-embrace,
finally exhibiting, as the journal puts it,
"severe and persistent
psychopathological behavior
of a depressive nature."

Now the question for the ape-gods was, how much
this was due to the room's size and form,
the length of the confinement,
the monkey's age, etc., etc.
So they tirelessly prepared, they report,
new combinations, new experiments.
And the question for the uninitiated:
What can this teach people?
How can this help people?
Do we learn here anything
more than what we already knew,
and knew too well?
Isn't this *l'art pour l'art?*
La psychologie pour la psychologie?
A gruesome game?

Financed by the National
Institute of Health.
Inconceivable.

But perhaps nevertheless conceivable—if one considers
how industrialized society has precisely,
as a simple by-product of its organization,
gradually and logically systematized mother deprivation—
if one sees the offerings for what they are, children
in the English coal mines' endless night,
laying-hens and veal-calves in windowless longhouses

in the countryside, latchkey children between highrises
and in slums—and if,
though it may be absurd, if the bitterest
of these experiments, the definitive
reduction of the fellowship of living things to nothing,
if it could be read as an attempt to find a cure for,
a serum against the apparently
incurable mother-need.

But it doesn't do that—
not even that.

3

Later, by the way,
the surrogate mother experiment achieved success.
This time she was upholstered with terrycloth
and outfitted with normal body heat
and the monkey baby held onto her neck
until she was suddenly cooled down
to a point near freezing
to simulate
maternal rejection.
The result was satisfactory:
"psychological death"
occurred.

"As flies to wanton boys,
are we to the gods;
they kill us for their sport,"
Shakespeare says.
Better to be a fly in a boy's hands,
a mortal in the hands of gods—
than to be a baby monkey
in these ape-gods' power.

PHOTOGRAPHS OF THE MEDUSA

Column six, page thirty-six
shows you goateed and smirking.
After thirteen years on death
row your stare still dares the camera,
unflinching and remorseless.
A fish knife to that girl's throat,
one hand fumbling your zipper,
when she thrashed under your heartbeat,
did you taste her blood, or your pleasure?
And you, freckled little boy
in aviator glasses,
when you waylaid a playmate
and bludgeoned him in the woods,
was it fun, like killing cats?
Was it like, the bases loaded,
you'd hit one out of the park?
And you, prosperous young shipping
company executive
whose eyes are snake eyes, too:
When you sent eight hundred tons
of milk powder unfit
for human consumption
to the Sudan, to feed
victims of famine,
did you count it a profit, or a thrill?

Pedophiles and parricides;
cannibals; perpetrators
of atrocities; inhuman,
evil celebrities; just
bad kids out for a good time:
Your reptile eyes confront mine
in the daily newspaper.
What is it you think you know
about yourselves, about me?

That I no longer wince? That
no ugliness is unimaginable?
That my heart is turning to stone?
And my God my shield, my only mirror,
is my own face looking back
with this simpleton love.

NO NO, BAD DADDY

A black pendulum, a dark tree unexplained, inexplicable.
A dark tree, a swinging shape, the nightmare comes and
comes. It's on the tip of memory, the lost line
of a favorite song. A death, someone lost? Whose are
those hands, loved? A dark shape, a black tree. Known hands
and this arm-deep thorn hedge, this riot of roses. Lovelier
in truth than legends say, shattering cobwebbed dusty glass
the sleeper sits up suddenly, her wide eyes stark. The new
puppy nuzzles her palm: A backyard limb grows a rope. This
is what will happen to you if you tell.
And what is there to say? We have become a nation of victims
and survivors, betrayed by fathers, teachers, coaches,
relatives, priests. Every few seconds in this nation I love
a child gasps awake, its scream sealed by an acid kiss.

NO WORST

The wicked stepmother bursts into her husband's
daughter's room, grabs a fistful of matted hair
and hauls the little bitch out of bed, late again.
The God-starved priest reaches gasping ecstasy
before a trembling fourteen-year-old carpenter's son.
And random ghouls roam, body-snatchers on the lookout
for children to rape. To torture. To murder. To devour.
The Mahatma wrote that the only true weapon
against evil is *Ahimsa*: nonviolence, love.
But how love the woman who holds a child's head
under the bath water? How love the man who stuffs
a wadded sock into his daughter's sobbing mouth? How,
no, don't ask for that, good Christ how shall I love
the Nosferatu behind the mask of a neighbor's face?

WOMAN KILLS AND EATS OWN INFANT

Tshew! Tshew! The kid's got a toy man whose limbs,
wrenched out in make-believe anger, expose easy-
to-pop-back-into bleeding holes. The old man's biting
the tip of his tongue over a hand-held video game,
scoring kicks to the testicles, kicks to the throat.
Still-life of the kitchen table: her mug and ashtray,
a box of rice, an onion, a pepper, a folded tabloid.
Cut. Aren't I as aesthetically anesthetized? Not yet
a sworn enemy of innocence, but as much a participant
in evil I do not choose? Turning pages, I collaborate
in someone's hi Mom moment of infamy, hold hands and leap
from the sure ground of normal experience into abysmal
freedom: to know the true horror: our infinite imagination,
our limitless capacity to do the worst we can conceive.

LIKE FATHER, LIKE SON

It comes over him sometimes, he can't help
it, it just comes over him and makes him want
something, want to do something, something
naughty. Something bad. And whose god's gonna
grab his wrist and spank the back of his hand,
whose god's gonna shake him to tooth chatter,
slap his face snotty, say you fucking little
piece of shit. Whose god's gonna make him be good?
Whose god will see him tiptoe into a dark room,
sit on a fragrant narrow bed, touch a dimpled arm,
awaken the little secret, and let it come over him?
Whose god cares enough to stop him? Where was your
god when he needed one? He's a piece of shit,
all right. Child of the only goddamned god he knows.

RILKE'S THIRD ELEGY
from the German

It's one thing to sing lovesongs. Another
the secret, guilty river-god of the blood.
Him she knows from afar, her love, what does he himself know
of the god of lust which so often roused him from the Alone,
before she could calm him, as though she didn't even exist,
raised, oozing what unknown, its own god-head,
rousing the night to endless uproar.
Oh the blood's Neptune, oh its terrible trident.
Oh the dark wind on his breast from that fluted nautilus.
Hear how the night hollows itself. You stars,
didn't the lover's desire for the loved one's face
begin in you? Didn't his inward insight
into her pure features come from your pure constellations?

Alas, not you nor his mother arched
the bow of his brow with such anticipation.
Not on yours, girl who loves him, did his lips
curve open to a gesture of fulfillment.
Do you really think your light touch
could shake him like this, you who waft like dawn-wind?
True, you tremble his heart, but older terrors
shook him with the tremor of feeling.
Call him . . . you don't call him completely away
from that dark company. Of course he wants to,
he does escape: released, he folds himself
to your innermost heart, takes and begins himself anew.
But did he begin himself, ever, really?
Mother, *you* made him, small; it was you who began him;
for you he was new, you arched the friendly world
over his new eyes, and deflected the world of strangers.
Where or where are the years when you could simply
place your slender body between him
and the rising flood of chaos?
How much you withheld from him thus;

you made the room of night terrors harmless,
from the sanctuary of your heart
you admixed human space into his night-space.
Not in the darkness, but in your nearness
you lit the night-light,
and it glowed like a friend.
There was no creak of the floor you couldn't explain
with a smile, as if you had known when it would come . . .

And he listened and was calmed. Your tender presence
in his room had such power: his tall, cloaked fate
slipped behind the dresser, and into the curtains' folds,
stirred by a breeze, his restless future molded itself.

And he himself, as he lay there relieved,
the sweetness of the safe world you had shaped
dissolving under his drowsy eyelids
into sleep he could almost taste—
he *seemed* protected . . . *Inside* him, though,
who could turn away, who could divert in him
the rising floods of origin?
Ah, there was no caution in that sleeper; sleeping,
but dreaming, but fevered: How he cast himself in!
He, the new, the timorous, how he was entangled
in the fast-growing thicket of inner event,
in twining patterns, a choking undergrowth
prowling with beasts. How he acquiesced—. Loved.
Loved his inner, his inner wildness,
this jungle within him; on mute fallen tree-trunks
his heart crowed, April green. Loved. Left it,
followed his own roots out to the mighty source
which already flowed beyond his little birth.
Loving, he waded deeper into the older blood,
down ravines where terror lay, glutted

with fathers. And each fear knew him,
winked as if in agreement.
Yes, the dreadful smiled . . . Seldom
did you smile so tenderly, Mother. How could he not
love it back, when it smiled. Before you
he had loved it, and in your womb,
it was dissolved in the waters that buoyed him.

Look: We don't love like flowers, only for
a single year; when we love
primordial sap rises in our arms. Girl,
this: that we love *inside* ourselves, not
the one of the presence becoming future, but
a countless brew of millions; not one child alone,
but the fathers who lie like broken mountain ranges
in our depths; but the dusty arroyos
of long-ago mothers—; but the entire
silent landscape under the cloudy or clear
sky of fate—: *this*, girl, preceded you.

And you yourself, what do you know—, you summoned up
prehistorical time in your lover. What passions
surged up inside him from the departed. What
women hated you there. What dark
men you aroused in your young man's veins. Dead
children reached toward you . . . Oh gently, gently,
for love of him do some simple, sure daily task,—
take him out near the garden, give him
power over the night . . .
                    Hold him back . . .

THE DEATH OF POLYXENA

from Euripides' Hecuba,
ca. *510ff.*

Hecuba:

> I am not to die.
> They deny me even this.
> My poor daughter,
> torn from my arms,
> joins my other children.
> O gods, gods.
>
> But tell me: How did she die?
> Was she slain with respect and honor,
> or terminated in a cold-eyed execution?
> I must know, though the knowledge
> flog me senseless.

Talthybius:

> I share your pain in the telling,
> for my telling doubles my tears:
> I wept once watching your daughter die,
> and I weep again, telling you.
>
> The entire army stood at attention
> as Achilles' son led Polyxena through their ranks
> and onto the grave. I stood near the tomb:
> I saw and heard it all. Behind her marched
> the young soldiers picked to be her guard.
>
> > Achilles' son raised a golden chalice
> and poured libation to his father's ghost.
> He signaled me to call for quiet.
> > "Attention! Attention!" I shouted.
> "Quiet, Achaeans! Silence in the ranks!"
> I heard a bird call.
> Then he began to pray.

"O son of Peleus, great Achilles, my father,
receive this wine as an invitation to return.
Rise, drink the wine you asked for:
our gift to you of the girl's blood.
Let us go now.
Let the winds come.
Give us homecoming.
Grant us safe return."

Thus he prayed, and the army prayed with him.
            Then,
drawing his golden-hilted sword,
he nodded to the guards
that they should seize her. But she spoke:

> "Wait, Greek pillagers
> of my city! I give you my death.
> I die of my own free will.
> Let no man touch me; I offer
> my raised throat to the blade.
> Free my hands so I can die free
> and be freed.
> I was a princess;
> I shall not die like a slave."

The army roared in approval,
and Agamemnon ordered the ropes cut.
In an instant, she ripped her tunic
from white shoulder to bright girdle,
baring gleaming breasts as lovely
as those of an alabaster goddess.
Then she sank to her knees, and spoke
her bravest words:

> "Soldiers,
> I present my breast to the sword.
> Or do you want my throat?
> Here: I yield it to you,
> Do what you must."

And for a moment, torn painfully
between admiration and duty,
Achilles' son hesitated.
Then he raised his sword
and brought it down
on the swan-curve of her throat.

HECUBA MOURNS

from Euripides' Hecuba,
ca. *585ff.*

Ah, my daughter:
which of this throng of griefs
demands most? I yield to one,
and they clamor around me,
each with its own heartbreak. Grief
after grief, a relentless tide of sorrows.
And with this last wave
I find myself drowning
in a sea of mother's tears.

        Even so, a cold comfort comes
        from knowing how free you were
        as you died.

Isn't it strange, how thistle ground
cultivated by the gods overflows
the granary, while the good soil the gods forget
grows a dry, uncombed tangle?
Human nature never changes:
the bad stay bad to the end;
the good, even touched by disaster,
are as changeless as stars.
            Are we born to our nature,
or is it something learned? Surely goodness
is a wise teacher. And a person well taught
comes to understand evil
by seeing the true beauty of the good.

        Ah, but these are the aimless arrows
        of despair.

[to Talthybius]

Go to the Greeks. Tell them that no one
is to touch my daughter. Have them hold
the crowds at bay.

For without tight-ship discipline,
armed men quickly kindle to violence.
And the one who is self-restrained
is called a yellow-bellied coward.

[to a young slave-woman]

Bring me a pitcher of seawater.
I must bathe my child for the last time,
for her burial wedding. For she is
death's loveliest bride.
What mother's keepsake of my own
can I give her? There is nothing left.
Nothing precious. Nothing loved.
      I'll ask the other slaves
whether something in their tents
has escaped the pilfering eye.
Some doodad someone has smuggled here,
some bright, contraband hope.

      Where has greatness gone?
Where has it gone, that airy palace
in which I was happy? My Lord Priam,
we once were blessed
with children and other wealth.
I was mother once,
now I am nothing.
All gone, my babies.

      And yet
we brag and strut like barnyard roosters;
the rich man so proud and contemptuous,
the politician gobbling great chunks
of the imaginary food of flattery.
We are so vain. Our lives are vain.
Happy are they who live between yesterday
and tomorrow. Happy are they

who ask for nothing: Their prayers
are the first to be answered.
Happy they whose luck lasts
for one single, blessed, eternal moment.

PROPOSITIONS

The soul grows hunched, flinching away from pain,
roaming through dank echoing corridors, learning not
to feel? Does that explain it? Two stunted souls
beget another in an unfeeling backseat tryst?
A soul-killing inherited virus is running amok?
A worst-contagion? A mutant chromosome? A dominant
or a recessive gene? Is it normal childhood anger,
disallowed? An interior pain-hobbled, foot-bound gait?
Some internal mark of Ham? A refusal to hope?
The generation's wit observes that good people
sleep better than bad, but the bad have much
more fun while they're awake. Do they?
Or are they so deeply seared they must wade out
into the river of flame to feel anything at all.

THE SACRAMENT OF POVERTY

for Judy Maines-La Marre

All the children on this ward are dying of AIDS.
The sister opens the door to two hundred and ten
quiet cribs lined in such tight ranks
you can barely squeeze between. This is not
an unpaid advertisement: You left your family,
the local value of your surname, your wind-tight house,
electricity, the safe water we turn on and drink,
and went for two weeks to Haiti,
to hold out your arms from a rocking-chair.
One by one babies were handed to you,
their skin smooth as black milk.
Gradually they remembered touch,
met your gaze, surrendered smiles.
One tottered through three wards to find you again;
he stood beside your chair, his cheek pressed to your arm.
All you can do, you said later, *is hold them
and love them. And let them go.*

And now this grief, Judy.
Each day another square to ex through.
You said you were helpless, dumb,
humbled by their pure poverty.
I never even started
your wedding poem.

(Magnificat)

LA PESTE

In the era of raining boys, a steady downpour
all shapes and sizes of Africans, Asians;
in the era of suicidal pleasure, of shooting-up
oblivion; in the era of handwringing research,
of children exing out father, mother, older sister,
neighbor, teacher, friend; in this era, they will say,
the worst epidemic by far was the gallop of evil
that overtook our kind like the virus from hell.
Its dragon breath passed from heart to heart,
engulfing whole continents with superiority, unwise
knowledge, and despair. It walked roughshod; it left
a black swath. But here we are, they will say,
shaking their heads with humble awe as others did
after the Black Death, after the Holocaust: Survivors.

Which reminds me of another knock-on-wood
memory. I was cycling with a male friend,
through a small midwestern town. We came to a 4-way
stop and stopped, chatting. As we started again,
a rusty old pick-up truck, ignoring the stop sign,
hurricaned past scant inches from our front wheels.
My partner called, "Hey, that was a 4-way stop!"
The truck driver, stringy blond hair a long fringe
under his brand-name beer cap, looked back and yelled,
      "You fucking niggers!"
And sped off.
My friend and I looked at each other and shook our heads.
We remounted our bikes and headed out of town.
We were pedaling through a clear blue afternoon
between two fields of almost-ripened wheat
bordered by cornflowers and Queen Anne's lace
when we heard an unmuffled motor, a honk-honking.
We stopped, closed ranks, made fists.
It was the same truck. It pulled over.
A tall, very much in shape young white guy slid out:
greasy jeans, homemade finger tattoos, probably
a Marine Corps boot-camp footlockerful
of martial arts techniques.

"What did you say back there!" he shouted.
My friend said, "I said it was a 4-way stop.
You went through it."
"And what did I say?" the white guy asked.
"You said: "'You fucking niggers.'"
The afternoon froze.

"Well," said the white guy,
shoving his hands into his pockets
and pushing dirt around with the pointed toe of his boot,
"I just want to say I'm sorry."
He climbed back into his truck
and drove away.

NOTES ON THE POEMS

I / MAMA AND DADDY

I had originally intended "Mama" of my second book, *Mama's Promises,* to be not only myself, my mother, and other mothers whose stories I snitched for the poems, but also the Divine Mother, the feminine face of God. Perhaps you will see that possibility in a few of the "Mama" poems. I wrote them when my son was a baby, though, and my own experience kept getting in the way.

"Emily Dickinson's Defunct" was written for my friend, feminist theologian Mary Pellauer, who once told me she found Dickinson "intimidating." My poem plays with that idea.

"The Fortunate Spill" is the true story of how my parents met: He crashed a New Year's Eve party and spilled black-eyed peas in her lap. She was a trained and intuitive pianist; that's why her forgetting five bars of music shocks her. The joke that makes both of them laugh is one her father used to tell.

"Epithalamium and Shivaree" is an occasional poem, written for a couple who bought my "poem-writing service" for $73 in a church auction, to be read at their wedding service.

I wrote "Light Under the Door" shortly after reading an article about children's fear of The Bomb. My father was a navigator on B-52s; he flew around with the bomb all the time. His crew was a lot like the crew of the bomber in *Dr. Strangelove* (1964), in which James Earl Jones plays the part of the navigator.

The Tuskegee Airmen stories are true. Bert Wilson spoke the best line in my book ("I was sleeping on his breath") over lunch one day while telling me his stories.

"I Am You Again" was written for one of my students, Hull Franklin, who "integrated"—the only Negro child in the school—a Mississippi elementary school in the 1960s. He was the most soft-spoken young man I've ever met. I hope he's learned to shout.

The family history poems are my mother's gift to me, and mine to her memory. In a dream once, while I was writing them, an antique telephone rang for me in my family's homeplace, and my great-grandfather told me his daughters were dreaming they were alive again because of me.

"Thus Far by Faith" is based on the early history of Thomas Chapel, a C.M.E. church in Hickman, Kentucky, whose first minister, Warren Thomas (born in 1812), was known as a slave to preach to mules. The final poems of the sequence describe the circumstances under which the church was formed.

III / Hermitage

"The Life of a Saint" was inspired by Giotto's frescoes about the life of St. Francis.

"I Dream the Book of Jonah" was inspired by my friend, Pamela Espeland, who, after reading the Book of Jonah in the Bible, suggested I try to write a poem about it. My Jonah is Mississippi John Hurt.

The "Abba Jacob" poems are inspired by a monk-priest who is my friend. They imitate the format of the apothegms of the Desert Fathers, the earliest Christian monks. Most of these poems are from my fourth book, *Magnificat*. The *Magnificat* is the prayer of Jesus' mother, Mary: "My soul proclaims the greatness of the Lord and my spirit exults in God my saviour; because he has looked upon his lowly handmaid. Yes, from this day forward all generations will call me blessed, for the Almighty has done great things for me. Holy is his name" (Luke 1:27–48). My using it as a title may be overreaching.

"Canticle for Abba Jacob" is an homage to "Canticle of the

Soul" by St. John of the Cross. The italicized passages are intended to echo the plainchant antiphons to the Virgin, whose Latin lyrics, about the longing of the soul for God, are from The Song of Songs.

Each of the poems of "The Plotinus Suite" was inspired by a passage from the *Enneads* of the neoplatonic philosopher Plotinus. Plotinus was the first Western philosopher to write about the mystical experience of Divine Union, which is the subject of my suite. "No Jazz," the first poem in the sequence, begins with an attempt to find a jazz station (fat chance) on the radio late at night in eastern Connecticut. "The Jesus Prayer" is the contemplative prayer Frannie is trying to practice in Salinger's *Frannie and Zooey.* You say "Lord Jesus Christ, have mercy on me" over and over, endlessly, until the noise of the mind is silenced and you hear the greater silence, the Silence of God. "Prayer of Singing Joy" begins with another contemplative practice, saying a mantra. Here the mantra becomes the tide. The final prayer described in this poem is what Catholics call the Prayer of the Saints, known popularly as "kything."

No, I am not Catholic.

IV / STILL FAITH

"Ape-Gods" is a translation from the Danish of Thorkild Bjørnvig. Bjørnvig has, since the 1950s, been considered by Denmark's leading critics to be a significantly distinguished poet. He is best known in his country for his memoir about his extraordinary relationship with Isaak Dinesen (Karen Blixen). Since the late 1970s, his poems have confronted environmental issues and animal rights.

The unbuttoned sonnets in this section were responses to my readings about the nature of radical evil from a bibliography prepared for me by my friend Lee Snook, professor of systematic theology at Luther Seminary.

The speeches from *Hecuba* are from my rendering of Euripides' play, which appears in *The Penn Greek Drama* series, edited by David Slavitt.

"The Sacrament of Poverty" was inspired both by my friend Judy Maines-La Marre and by Abba Jacob's saying that poverty is a sacrament if it humbles us to the realization that we are all poor.

"Minor Miracle" describes an experience I had in the early 1970s. It is a true story.

INDEX OF TITLES AND FIRST LINES

Titles of poems are in italics, first lines in Roman type. If titles and first lines are identical or nearly so, only the title is given.

206

208